Postwar South Korea
and
Japanese Popular Culture

By

Sungmin Kim

Postwar South Korea
and
Japanese Popular Culture

By

Sungmin Kim

TRANS
PACIFIC
PRESS

SENGO KANKOKU TO NIHON BUNKA: "WASHOKU" KINSHI KARA "HANRYU" MADE by Sungmin Kim
© 2014 by Sungmin Kim
Originally published in 2014 by Iwanami Shoten, Publishers, Tokyo.
This English edition published 2023
by Trans Pacific Press Co., Ltd., Tokyo
by arrangement with Iwanami Shoten, Publishers, Tokyo

Trans Pacific Press Co., Ltd.
2nd Floor, Hamamatsu-cho Daiya Building
2-2-15 Hamamatsu-cho, Minato-ku,
Tokyo 105-0013, Japan
Telephone: +81-(0)50-5371-9475
Email: info@transpacificpress.com
Web: http://www.transpacificpress.com

Edited by Karl Smith, Melbourne, Australia.
Designed and set by Ryo Kuroda, Tsukuba-city, Ibaraki, Japan.

Distributors

USA, Canada and India
Independent Publishers Group (IPG)
814 N. Franklin Street
Chicago, IL 60610, USA
Telephone inquiries: +1-312-337-0747
Order placement: 800-888-4741 (domestic
only)
Fax: +1-312-337-5985
Email: frontdesk@ipgbook.com
Web: http://www.ipgbook.com

Europe, Oceania, Middle East and Africa
EUROSPAN
Gray's Inn House,
127 Clerkenwell Road
London, EC1R 5DB
United Kingdom
Telephone: +44-(0)20-7240-0856
Email: info@eurospan.co.uk
Web: https://www.eurospangroup.com

Japan
MHM Limited
3-2-3F, Kanda-Ogawamachi, Chiyoda-ku,
Tokyo 101-0052
Tel: +81-3-3518-9181
Fax: +81-3-3518-9523
Email: sales@mhmlimited.co.jp
Web: http://www.mhmlimited.co.jp

China
China Publishers Services Ltd.
718, 7/F., Fortune Commercial Building,
362 Sha Tsui Road, Tsuen Wan, N.T.
Hong Kong
Telephone: +852-2491-1436
Email: edwin@cps-hk.com

Southeast Asia
Alkem Company Pte Ltd.
1, Sunview Road #01-27, Eco-Tech@Sunview
Singapore 627615
Telephone: +65 6265 6666
Email: enquiry@alkem.com.sg

The publication of this book was supported by a Grant-in-Aid for Publication of Scientific Research Results (Grant Number 21HP6003), provided by the Japan Society for the Promotion of Science, to which we express our sincere appreciation.

ISBN 978-1-876843-74-8 (hardback)
ISBN 978-1-876843-80-9 (paperback)
ISBN 978-1-876843-86-1 (eBook)

Table of Contents

List of Images

List of Tables

Preface to the English edition

This book explores the cultural relationship between Japan and South Korea after World War II, focusing on transnational cultural flows of media and popular culture, a perspective which has not been fully elucidated in either modern Japanese studies or modern Korean studies. The chronological focus of this book covers approximately 60 years, which can be classified into three distinct periods: 1945–65, 1965–late-80s, and late-80s–mid-2000s. The key turning points in this history of cultural relationships are: 1945, when South Korea was liberated from its colonial rule following Japan's defeat in World War II; 1965, when Japan and South Korea normalized diplomatic relations; during the subsequent period various political and economic relations were established between the two countries under the Cold War regime; the end of the 1980s, when geopolitical conditions in East Asia changed dramatically and East Asia political and market liberalization began in earnest; the early 2000s, when the globalization of the media and popular culture accelerated. In the historical context spanning 60 years, I have tried to shine a light on "culture" as a historical experience in which national, local, and global movements are intricately inter-twined, an experience which has sometimes been excluded from Japan–Korea relations and sometimes hidden from people's daily lives.

To this end, this book focuses on media and popular culture, which constitute a crucial social space (arena) that most visibly tracks the changes in Japan–South Korean relations wrought by the amalgam of postcolonialism and postmodernism, industrialization and democra-tization, internationalization, informatization, the transformation of geopolitics during and after the Cold War and the expansion of markets called globalization. What has been built in that space is not Japan–South Korea relations in the narrow sense that national surveys measure in reductive schema such as "pro-Japanese", "anti-Japanese", "pro-Korean", or "anti-Korean", but Japan–Korea relations in a broad sense that are actively developed in the intertwining of individual desires with the fusion and production of culture in which the local and global intersect.

From this perspective, the relationship between Japan and South Korea appears as a vital historical experience that transcends a simple bilateral diplomatic and political relationship – one that intersects the multiple dimensions of the national, the regional and the global.

When this book was originally published in Japan in 2014, the relationship between Japan and South Korea was described as the worst it had been since WWII. In the context of still-unresolved historical issues about colonial domination, accelerated economic competition due to Japan's decline and South Korea's growth, an increasingly Cold-War-like tension in East Asia due to China's rapid growth, and so forth, politicians and the mass media inflamed nationalism to a level in which mutual hatred pervaded everyday life. This situation has not changed, even since 2017 when the Korean edition was published. Indeed, that antagonism and tension has extended into the economic relationship that Japan and Korea have built. Furthermore, rather than improving the "worst relationship since-WWII", recent moves have been made which take such antagonism and tension for granted.

However, if we scrutinize the present Japan–South Korea relations from the perspective of media and popular culture, a completely different relationship appears. The two countries now share a huge market and a common cultural space that transcends mere production and consumption, starting with K-pop, which became a global phenomenon in the late 2010s, and centering on South Korean television dramas, films, webtoons, novels, and food culture. Young people disillusioned with the mass media have established cultural relations through social media and global platforms.

This shift indicates precisely how multilayered Japan–South Korea relations are. As I demonstrate in this book, the cultural relationship between Japan and South Korea in the "1965 system" was based on Japanese popular culture, even as Korea imposed bans on that very culture in an effort to address unequal power relations. Considered from that angle, the present Japan–South Korea cultural relationship is centered around historical experiences of South Korean popular culture, even while perpetuating the worst political relationship premised upon equal power relations.

How should we understand the multilayered Japan–Korea relationship? This book provides a vantage point and frame for understanding not merely its history until 2004, but also in the present continuous tense. Its significance is, I suspect, one of the reasons for the publication of this English edition eight years after the first edition, and I am wholeheartedly delighted. Through this book, I would certainly like to continue discussion with many readers.

In writing this volume, I received enormous help and advice from my academic advisor Professor Myung-koo Kang and my fellow researchers under his supervision in the Department of Communication, Seoul National University, where I completed my Master's degree; and my academic advisor Professor Shunya Yoshimi and my fellow researchers in the Graduate School of Interdisciplinary Information Studies, University of Tokyo, where I received my Doctorate. My capacity to imagine "Japan and Korea as historical experience" expanded through debate with them.

Many people aided in the process of publication. This book owes its existence to Mr. Yoshizumi Higuchi, editor at Iwanami Shoten, whose untiring efforts made it a work that could appeal to a wider readership; to Geulhangari Publishers, which published the South Korean edition; to Professor Yoshio Sugimoto and Ms Yuko Uematsu of Trans Pacific Press who undertook to publish this English edition; to Dr Leonie Stickland and Dr. Karl Smith, who translated and edited the complex content; and to the readers who have perused its previous versions. I also thank my colleagues and students at Hokkaido University to which I am affiliated; the Japan Society for the Promotion of Science from which I received funding for the publication of the English edition; and the researchers and readers who have shown interest in this study and have interacted with me.

Finally, I dedicate this volume to my family in South Korea and Japan, who supported me from my birth in Seoul and during my journey via Tokyo to my current home in Sapporo, Japan.

February 2023
Sungmin Kim

Introduction: The age of the ban and Japan–Korea Relations

The Japanese–Korean 1965 System and the ban on Japanese popular culture

Ujusonyeon Atom (*Astro Boy*) is the Korean title of the Japanese television animated cartoon, *Tetsuwan Atomu* (Steel-arm Atom). In the 1970s and '80s, children in South Korea, including the author, grew up not with *Tetsuwan Atomu*, but with *Ujusonyeon Atom*.[1] However, until the late 1990s, when the fact that *Astro Boy* was a Japanese-made robot became widely known in Korea, *Astro Boy* was perceived to have been made in Korea. On television, the theme song was in Korean, and the toy that emerged when the hatch in the abdomen was opened had the clear imprint of Korean Hangul script. Moreover, Korea's most popular soccer player Hong Myung-bo played for the Pohang Atoms. Nevertheless, until the 1990s, when Japanese cultural goods began to be officially imported, importing *Tetsuwan Atomu* was prohibited. In its place, *Ujusonyeon Atom* flew the skies of Korea, where rapid economic growth coincided with a military dictatorship.

Rather than being exceptional, this case of *Ujusonyeon Atom* might be seen as representative of the traffic in cultural products through different phases of the Japan–Korea relationship in the late twentieth century, and especially after the 1965 normalization of diplomatic relations. This example highlights the mechanisms by which "prohibition" and "trans-bordering" continually coexisted during the decades-long "ban on Japanese popular culture", a dynamic that cannot be fully explained in terms of the history of formal Japan–Korea relations which treats the so-called "opening-up of Japanese popular culture" in 1998 as a turning-point between cultural isolation and open exchange.

Japan–Korea relations in the twentieth century were formed by two systems, namely, colonial domination by the former Japanese Empire until 1945, and the so-called 1965 System from 1965, following

---

1 Throughout this book, numerous works are cited which, like *Astro Boy*, have titles in three languages. For ease of reading, in most cases only the English title is presented in the text. All works cited are listed in the Appendix, where the interested reader can find the Korean and Japanese titles tabulated alongside the English title.

the signing of the Treaty on Basic Relations between Japan and the Republic of Korea. In contrast to colonialism, which was effectively a bilateral relationship under the imperial order between Japan and Korea, the structure of the 1965 System was far more complex. Aligned in the Cold War with the overwhelming power that was America,[2] Japan the former colonizer and Korea the formerly colonized continued to (re)structure their postcolonial relationship as friendly nations that, on the one hand, cooperated with one another in the competition between the regimes of East and West for industrial modernization, while on the other hand were troublesome neighbors who continued to dispute the history of the colonial period. The fierce resistance to the normalization of relations between Japan and the Republic of Korea still leaves a multitude of diverse problems today, indicating the complex difficulties of the 1965 System.

The cultural character of this 1965 System has scarcely been elucidated. Although there has been much discussion around the politics and economic relationships of the 1965 System, issues of culture – and especially popular culture – which were excised from those discussions were left as near-blanks. However, as the case of *Ujusonyeon Atom* demonstrates, even during the so-called "prohibition" prior to 1988, when a "new Japan–Republic of Korea partnership towards the twenty-first century" was announced by Japanese Prime Minister Obuchi Keizō and South Korean President Kim Dae-jung and the ban on Japanese cultural content in Korea was lifted (hereafter, termed the "opening-up of Japanese popular culture"), Korean society and Japanese popular culture had been in continuous contact in various ways. For many Koreans, experiences of Japanese comics (*manga*) and animation (*anime*), films, novels and so on were not only enshrined in their individual memories, but were part of a collective memory that ran through certain different communities and generations. In other words, it is impossible to understand Japanese–Korean postwar

---

2   It is worth noting that while it is a long-standing and widespread convention to refer to the United States of America with the shorthand "America" and its citizens as "Americans", this terminology is problematic in that it excludes all of the other peoples who are also Americans, from Canada to Chile. However, since there is no easy solution to this problem, we will continue to follow this convention throughout this volume.

cultural relations without examining the inextricable interplay between the ban on Japanese popular culture and border-crossing in the history of popular culture.

The scope of the ban on Japanese popular culture

Debates so far appear neither to have linked the ban on Japanese popular culture with cultural relations between Japan and Korea, nor to have sufficiently understood its nature. This is probably because they have only considered this issue in terms of the universal sense inherent in the banning of the inflow of culture. The task of "bordering," motivated by fears of cultural influence from large neighboring political entities, and endeavoring to prevent its permeation, is a kind of universal identity politics that frequently occurs in the process of state-formation. In the latter half of the twentieth century, dozens of countries, mainly in Asia and Africa, achieved independence, even as the world experienced a simultaneous acceleration in the spread of mass media and capitalist culture from the dominant powers, centering on America. The "trans-bordering" of media and popular culture has thus been understood as a grave problem for the independence of emerging nations concerned about cultural domination by others. The concept of cultural imperialism gained traction in the 1960s, being an accumulation of experiences, perceptions and emotions around the postwar cultural order and particularly around the increasingly globalized media space.

At this point, we might be tempted to define the ban on Japanese popular culture, first, as "postcolonial identity politics" and protectionism in the interests of building a media culture and national identity centered on the formation and diffusion of television broadcasting. The cultural influence of the former colonizer was perceived to be a cultural threat reminiscent of the violent cultural suppression and control it had exercised during the colonial period. However, when one considers the intimate political and economic relationships between Japan and Korea, a variety of experiences that run counter to identity politics remain unexplained. Hence, this definition is not sufficient to explain the ban on Japanese popular culture until 1998.

Various historical and geopolitical conditions in postwar Japan and Korea are missing from here. For example, what was the influence of the Cold War and America in determining the cultural characteristics of Korean society? What was the influence of the tension with North Korea on national mobilization and industrial modernization under a developmental dictatorship? Questions such as these appear to have been excluded from previous attempts to explain the "Japan–Korea" frame solely in terms of the colonial legacy.

Debates hitherto have attempted to grasp the coexistence of prohibition and cultural traffic, accepting the ban at face value, without first questioning the state of that very "ban". Such assumptions create binary frames such as legal versus illegal, permissible versus infringing, subordination versus resistance, and so forth. Once framed as such, experiences have been interpreted as being mere infringement or subordination, or reducible to some disposition, such as the "duality of the formerly colonized." One result of such framing is that, in Korea, the colonial times have been spoken of as "memories we want to forget" from prior to the "Korean Wave" ("*Hallyu*"), while in Japan there is a widespread perception of Korean backwardness which underpins "anti-Korean discourse", which in turn is seen as the only explanation necessary.

Drawing a line under such explanations and understandings, this book seeks to critically examine the ban on Japanese popular culture and situate it as the most revealing evidence of the cultural dynamism of the postwar relationship between Japan and Korea. This book takes the view that the ban on Japanese popular culture was a historical construct born of various geopolitical conditions in Japan, Korea, and East Asia more broadly, which symbolizes the twisted cultural relationships between the two nations. In other words, this book will focus on the experiences of prohibition and trans-bordering around Japanese popular culture in Korea, to shed light on the dynamic cultural relationship between Japan and Korea through the process in which the ban was constructed (Part One); its mechanism (Part Two); and the process of its dismantling (Part Three).

Motivation for the ban on Japanese popular culture

In order to elucidate the nature of the ban on Japanese popular culture and the process of its implementation, as well as the various cultural products in that process, there is a need to draw a line between earlier perspectives that have positioned the ban on Japanese popular culture as a soundly "legal thing" whose nature is part of a "task of decolonization", and as something fluid and productive formed in the contentious dynamic between the global and the local; between ambivalence and the hybridity inherent in the formation of nations; in the various cultural relationships in East Asia that formed during the Cold War; and between the discord and desire produced by the processes of decolonization and modernization.

A state continuously constructs and reshapes its national identity through a process of defining and redefining borders in its interactions with heterogeneous others (Cohen 1994: 1) by way of sustaining cultural differences between groups. In other words, bordering is a process of defining a social partition, even while destabilizing trans-bordering is continually accommodated (Barth 1969: 16).

In contemporary society, mass media has become the most important factor in that bordering. The term "media space" will be frequently used in this book as a more accurate expression than the term "cultural space" to refer to a space where various discourses, practices and systems pertaining to the creation of national identity compete, such as the formation of state information systems centered upon the mass media and the preservation of national culture, the production of a common ideology, and so forth (Schlesinger 1987: 239–242).

However, with the globalization of media in contemporary society, it is both systematically and technically impossible to prohibit an other's culture and completely prevent transnational cultural border-crossing (Collins 1990).

For example, in Ireland, which experienced seven centuries of colonization by Britain, post-colonial nationalism took the form of "de-Anglicization" alongside a discourse of cultural imperialism grounded in fear of the influence of magazines, films, television, radio and popular music imported from Britain, which continued to shape the Irish discourse around the media and its system for decades (Tovey &

Share 2000: 419). However, during a period of rapid economic growth from the 1960s into the 1970s, many Irish people acquired their sense of modernization from imported radio and television programming, including from the British Broadcasting Corporation (BBC). The Irish government at the time tacitly consented to the influx of British popular culture through broadcast spillover and the like because, while protecting Ireland from British culture was an important tool of identity politics, cultural trans-bordering was simultaneously a means to influence both opening the economy and commercializing the mass media (Barbrook 1992: 208–210). This dynamic was not limited to a few countries but impacted most countries (especially former colonies) that have neighbors with large cultural influence. In other words, the diffusion of media and popular culture since World War II has largely ensured that national cultures are continuously exposed to the outside under processes of modernization, are thus weakened through cultural impact and permeation, and are incapable of preserving distinct national identities.

Accordingly, the media space in which identity politics are conducted is not a closed space in which a country's culture is rigidly protected from foreign cultures, but rather a permeable space which is constantly exposed to foreign cultures. Anxiety and fear – an "identity crisis" (Hall 1992) – caused by the perceived threat of foreign culture are experienced as "communal issues" (Morley & Robins 1995: 287–288), and construct identity politics in the media space. In other words, identity politics in a postcolonial media space refers to a process of bordering, that is, identity formation, a process constantly at risk from a contradictory process of trans-bordering, that is, "identity-loss" (Bhabha 1994). This "postcolonial dilemma" (Hutcheon 1989) fundamentally determines the ambivalence at the core of the "ban".

Defining the ban on Japanese popular culture

In this book, I therefore wish to establish as a starting point an understanding of the ban on Japanese popular culture as an "ambivalent model that was not enshrined in law."

Laws are legislation created by a state along with the various criteria necessary for the government and/or administrative authority

6

to implement them. From Max Weber's classification of the types of norms as "statutes", "traditions", and "morality," the ban on Japanese popular culture was not a written statute, but more like a convention or tradition "guaranteed by the probability that deviant action will be met by physical or psychic coercion aimed to compel conformity or to punish disconformity by a staff specialized for this purpose" (Weber 1922=1972). However, the coexistence of prohibition and trans-bordering over several decades cannot be fully explained as merely a convention. Although there was social sharing of understanding and sentiment around the legitimacy of the ban on Japanese popular culture, the concrete means and methods aimed at implementing the ban were maintained for several decades in an extremely ambiguous condition.

In this context, this book will not venture to offer a singular definition of the ban on Japanese popular culture but will seek to define it as a "historical construct in which multiple social forces conflict and contradict", whose meaning is determined according to what or who guarantees its legitimacy. Based on this thinking, motivations for the ban on Japanese popular culture can be grouped into the following four points:

1. Departure from the cultural influence of the former colonizer (decolonization)

2. Local struggle against the globalization of mass media (critique of cultural imperialism)

3. Economic strategy as an independent emerging nation pursuing development (industrial modernization)

4. Multi-layered operation of authority through public and private censorship (nationalization)

Various studies in fields such as cultural anthropology and sociology, psychoanalysis, media and culture studies, and postcolonial theory have explored the cultural processes of bordering in communities (Kim 2013), but this kind of grouping is, to the last, one that has been derived from the phenomena dealt with in this book. Without defining these four justifications as a single model, this book has listed them as is because for the surrounding countries in the postwar era, the various cultural norms involved in the process of constructing their identity were always entangled in a complex manner, and in conflict and contradiction, regardless of how much the state had become the exemplar. To express this in another way, the universality of a "ban" itself acquires its distinctiveness by means of these four justifications.

Through the state of the legal system, media practice and social discourse, this book will elucidate the mechanism of the ban on Japanese popular culture in a media space where these four justifications were intricately intertwined. The ban on Japanese popular culture was a historical process that was constructed, implemented and dismantled amid various geopolitical conditions involving postwar Japan and Korea. By focusing upon that process of construction, implementation and dismantling, I aim to shed light upon the various experiences and memories that cannot be explained in binary terms such as legal versus illegal, permitted versus infringing, and subordination versus resistance.

Of course, the media and popular culture were not the only spheres undergoing this sort of de-Japanization in post-independence Korea. In the academic space, too, for example, the construction of new knowledge was accomplished through multilayered "borders" such as those between Japan and America, the global and the local, decolonization and modernization, and socialism and capitalism, which has in turn given rise to all manner of contradictions. This book focuses on popular culture in Japan and Korea because the media and popular culture have constituted a space where people consciously or unconsciously compete in the most complicated manner, where repression and desire around Korea's "dream of modernity" cannot be reduced to a task of decolonization as "nationals". In other words, by examining media and popular culture products in which American, Japanese and Korean formats and themes, principles and common sense have been blended together in complex ways, we can consider how various experiences and memories that cannot be reduced simplistically to "us" and "them" defined by national borders have shaped Korean modernity.

Moreover, such a study will also shed light on the situation in Japan and Korea today, where we see an unprecedented "amity" that has spread through the media and popular culture, and again an unprecedented "antipathy" that is arguably a backlash against it. The roller-coaster-like cultural relationship between Japan and Korea did not suddenly begin with the World Cup and *Hallyu* but has been built with much conflict and all kinds of popular culture throughout the twentieth century, and thus most things are shared problems experienced through the postwar and post-independence frames. In other words, it is the aim of this book to restructure the official history that is riddled with misunderstanding and ignorance, apathy and forgetting; to clarify the historical process which produced the Japan–Korea cultural relationship and its mechanisms; and to drive even the smallest crack into the mutually tenacious political imagination and belief that has relied upon excessive nationalism.

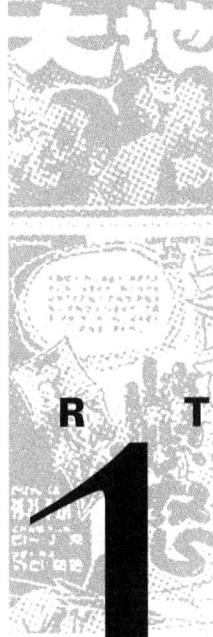

01

Historical conditions of the Korean ban on Japanese popular culture

This section considers how Japanese style and the Cold War shaped the postwar relationship between Korean society and Japanese culture

Chapter 1

"JAPANESE STYLE" AND THE BAN

The "ban on Japanese popular culture" highlights the multiple layers of the post-colonial situation in Korea. In this chapter we will examine how this ban on Japanese culture was created after the Japanese withdrawal from Korea. What was prohibited, and what permitted? At the root of these questions lies the term *waesaek*, or "Japanese style."

The origin of the ban on Japanese popular culture

The landscape of the "liberation space" and "Japanese style" (*waesaek*)

"Bordering on Chaos," an expression which appears in Volume VI of the 1948 *Foreign Relations of the United States* (hereafter *FRUS*) series, concisely depicts the Korean "liberation space" in just two words: "bordering" – interpreted more broadly than the mere drawing of borders – and "chaos." In the unstable and confused situation between the liberation of the Korean Peninsula which began with Japan's surrender on 15 August 1945, the Republic of Korea was defined by a variety of borders, beginning with the North/South divide by the United States of America and the Soviet Union from 9 September 1945 until the establishment of an independent government on 15 August 1948, after three years of American military government (AMG) administration.

As will be discussed in detail in Chapter Two, the process of border-formation or "bordering" in this three-year liberation space was not limited to drawing national borders. Its moves were an omen of the

Cold War, comprising both "the political" (Schmitt 1932), made up of enemies centering upon the Soviet Union and friends pivoting upon the U.S., and "the cultural" (Buck-Morss 2002), in which the task of continuing to define those friends and enemies was deeply connected to issues of identity. While the north went on to set up a communist state under the Soviet Union's military control, in the south, under the direction of U.S. forces, communism was thoroughly eliminated, and U.S.-style democracy was embraced.

The job of creating cultural borders vis-à-vis Japan, the former colonizer, was an important challenge in the "liberation space." Many intellectuals advocated erasing all traces of "Japanization" from the colonial period to achieve cultural independence, as a way of sloughing off the cultural control of the colonial period when the Japanese empire had imposed bans and censorship on public opinion and popular culture (plays, gramophone recordings, films, publications, entertainment, exhibitions, advertisements, and so on), symbolized by the prohibition on use of the Korean language. The Japanese language and Japanese (-style) culture were identified as the primary cultural symbols of that Japanization.

The nurturing and growth of culture is, in short, the pride of the people, and the quintessence of their daily existence. Formerly, the Japanese empire, fearing the results of such great progress, were intent upon and concerned to erase everything connected with culture in colonized Korea... and, by severing Korea and the Korean people's every last cultural artery, strove for total fulfilment of their political ambitions... Thanks to liberation ... we have reclaimed our language and taken back our surnames. (*The Kyunghyang Shinmun* 1948)

Image 1.1: A sign with Japanese lettering as a vestige of *waesaek* (*The Kyunghyang Shinmun* 1947a)

The term "*waesaek*" was used to indicate vestiges of Japanization. Colonial-era signs and trademarks, use of Japanese language by the general public, and records and films, et cetera, were dubbed "Japanese style," and were removed or confiscated as "elements that have seemed to compromise the clarity of national being" (Morley & Robins 1995: 189). One newspaper described this as a process of "rapidly jettisoning colonial-period customs and becoming members of a new nation" (*The Dong-A Ilbo* 1948).

The meaning of the negative and multi-layered word "*wae*" can be traced to the "*waegu*" (*wae* = Japanese; *gu* = pirates or bandits) of Goryeo and Joseon times, indicating Japanese and other foreigners who invaded between the thirteenth and fifteenth centuries. According to Morisaki Kazue, as damage from "*waegu*" progressively worsened, the concept came to refer to a process of change in the East Asian geopolitical situation concerning China, Japan, Ryūkyū (the present-day Okinawa), and Korea from the thirteenth century, when a ban was imposed on "*wajin*", and negotiations were conducted with Japan on how to handle the "*waegu*" (Morisaki 1971).

In those circumstances, fear that their borders would be encroached by "Japanese" and Koreans' feelings of cultural supremacy over those "Japanese" dominated the sentiments of the people of the Korean peninsula towards *waegu*. After experiencing a violently repressive colonial regime, these sentiments manifested as hostility and fear towards Japanese imperialism, as well as feelings of cultural supremacy vis-à-vis Japan, and self-esteem (Yoo 1998: 446).[1] The term *waesaek*, which evokes the colonial period, was a keyword symbolizing danger, impurity and misfortune which violate the subjectivity of the nation.

---

1   According to Jeon Jaeho, who discusses the formation of Korean society with a focus on the Park regime, ordinary Koreans have hitherto considered that until premodern times, the Korean Peninsula was politically and culturally superior to the Japanese archipelago, but as Korea (Joseon) was unable to respond adequately to encroachment from the West, it began to fall behind Japan, eventually becoming a Japanese colony. Such ideas greatly contributed to strengthening the Korean people's ethnic consciousness and identity. In short, he argues that feelings of cultural supremacy vis-à-vis Japan and the experience of colonial domination made "anti-Japanese ideology" an important element of post-independence Korean nationalism (Jeon 2002: 130).

Contradictions around the prohibition of Japanese style

The basic motivation for the ban on Japanese popular culture was Korea's nation-building program (Williams 2004: 55–60) – the quest for cultural and social homogenization in the "liberation space" to form a nation anew after independence from the Japanese empire. Conventionalization and traditionalization as sustained interaction (including prohibition) with the Other, the Foreigner, and the Invader – with any external culture which encroaches upon a cultural border – are the primary methods of border-formation (Cohen 1994; Freud 2001).

In South Korea, the process of border-creation was mainly directed at North Korea and Japan, focused on the question of "what to choose as being homogeneous with the nation and its people." The program of nation-building that "othered" North Korea involved not only countering the enemy (communist forces) beyond the 38th parallel, but also labelling people within its borders as communists and unpatriotic, and targeting them for extermination and exclusion, including the use of physical force such as detention and massacre. Numerous incidents prior to the outbreak of the Korean War, such as the "April 3 Uprising and Massacre" on Jeju Island (April 1948) and the "Yeosu-Suncheon Incident" (October 1948), indicate the extent of violence deployed in "bordering" against communism within South Korea.

In contrast, as suggested by the newspaper article in Image 1.2, bordering against Japan was primarily cultural. Where bordering vis-à-vis North Korea sought the elimination of communist bodies, bordering vis-à-vis Japan sought to cleanse each Korean "national" of the marks of Japanization which had been inscribed on their bodies during the colonial period (Lee 2008b: 388).

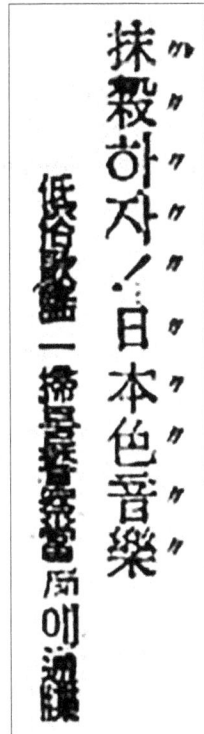

Image 1.2: A newspaper article advocating eradication of *waesaek* music (*The Dong-A Ilbo* 1946)

The streets are still brimming with Japanese songs whose lyrics have simply been changed to our language. The main ones being sung here and there without modification have militaristic or blues-style decadent lyrics and melodies. Nothing is so sad or shameful. What is more, while the Training Bureau of the Department of Education places emphasis upon music education, and preparation is underway for the institution of refined and innovative music, on the other hand in the Department of Police Affairs, they have decided to crack down stringently, instructing each of the police agencies under their jurisdiction to rid all theaters, coffee shops, musical instrument stores and the like of vulgar songs without fail. (*The Dong-A Ilbo* 1946)

This systematic program of eradicating Japanese style was formalized after the government of the Republic of Korea was established on 15 August 1948, and the inauguration of the first Syngman Rhee regime. The government, police and city authorities were proactive, with President Rhee declaring, for instance, "[We] must prevent flooding of the market by Japanese manufactured goods: I will punish Department of Internal Affairs officials in the event of their failure" (*The Chosun Ilbo* 1954). For the Rhee regime, anti-Japanese nationalism was a potent means of strengthening the regime's nationalistic image under the circumstances of a nation divided in the process of its foundation.

Promotion of elimination of *waesaek*: now, seven years since liberation from the Japanese Empire, vestiges of Japanese language still remain in everyday terminology, nameplates in commercial quarters, and so on; and because this is a huge disgrace, public and private jointly need to coordinate their efforts for a national spiritual purification movement. (*The Kyunghyang Shinmun* 1952)

After the Korean War, more systematic regulation was attempted in each field of "popular culture." Anti-Japanese censorship laws and ordinances were instituted in 1955, including "The matter of scripts in relation to films and plays," "Film censorship guidelines," "Presentation on the direction of foreign film policy," "Original plan for film censorship standards," "Temporary measures bill relating to foreign film importation," and "Domestic record production and record censorship standards for recordings imported from foreign countries," as well as controls on importation of publications, films and records, and the seizure of books and goods that were in circulation.

In films, the "imitation of Japanese films," "Japanese language," and the "Cinematization of Japanese costumes and customs" were defined as *waesaek*, and were subject to censorship (Lee 2009a: 416–424). In 1958, for example, the first warning notice that the Department of Education sent to the "Guild of Korean Screenwriters" was about *waesaek* (*The Kyunghyang Shinmun* 1959).

> Of course, [you] must not imitate or plagiarize Japanese works, nor cinematize *waesaek* unless it is unavoidable for the purpose of elevating national spirits.
>
> 1. Even in the case where it is for the raising of national vitality, [we] forbid the use of more than one passage of Japanese language.
>
> 2. [You] absolutely must refrain from cinematization of Japanese costumes and customs.
>
> 3. [We] forbid *waesaek* music for sound effects.

However, throughout the Rhee regime, the program to eliminate Japanese style was increasingly unable to be justified solely in terms of decolonization. The reason for this was the meagre legitimacy of the Rhee regime: while that regime aggressively employed a nationalist discourse which merged anti-communist and anti-Japanese sentiments to become a discursive apparatus for building conformity and patriotic "members of the nation." it also appointed colonial collaborators to key positions in the state apparatus (Lim 2000: 198–199). The poet Ko Un borrowed from the life of Kim Jeong-ryeol, who continued to rise through the ranks for several decades after the end of the Japanese empire, and wrote his profile in the form of a poem.

Attended the Imperial Army Academy
in Japanese imperial times;
Company Commander of the Japanese Army Air Corps;
As Air Combat Admiral,
fought the American Naval Air Squadron;
Survived that midair combat;
When liberation came,
After hiding for a while,
Appears in the founding of the national military,
Crossing from yonder hill to this hill here;
Becomes inaugural Chief of the General Staff
in the Korean Air Force;
Becomes friends with the U.S. military
that once were foes;
Chef de Mission, United Nations Command in Korea;
Becomes last Director of the Department of National Defense
in the Liberal Party government;
At night, meets Consuls from the U.S. Embassy; and
Drinks at the house of the Cheongwa-dong Official Appraiser;
In the morning, visits the Speaker, Lee Ki-poong
and presents his compliments;
In the daytime, is called to the national parliament building, and
Jeers at questions from Opposition members;
Calls citizens who demonstrate insurgents, and
Calls them Reds;
Opposition members snatch the rostrum mike.

Even after those times, the era of Syngman Rhee has passed,
Kim becomes Park Chung-hee's first
Republican Party President of Parliament;
Chairs the Anti-communist League;
Is National Constituency Republican member; and
Later advances to the business world
And to the corporate community.
Ten years of economic activity.
Along with the launch of the government of
Chun Doo-hwan's military regime, becomes

Executive Vice-Chair of the National Unification Advisory Council;
and
Chun Doo-hwan's last Prime Minister.
Heads the Roh Tae-woo regime's Korea–Japan Cooperation
Committee.
Why so long, long-serving?
Why so safe,
With not a jot of remorse?
Why such success,
With not a jot of pain?

Heedless of the dark clouds of the folk of this land,
Their sorrow like bloody pus,
Why does he have such a bright, shining face? (Ko 2006: 43–44)

In the end, if we understand "decolonization" as being "efforts to save or restore the sense and fact of [the] community" (Said 1993: 252–253) called Korea against the colonial regime, then Rhee's cultural politics – which personally and structurally inherited the vestiges of Japanese imperialism even while touting anti-Japanese sentiments and expanding conflict with the colonial collaborators called the "pro-Japanese group" – cannot be fully explained as decolonization. As sociologist Kim Dong-chun points out: "[t]he anomie seen in contemporary Korea can be found in pro-Japanese personnel" (Kim 2000: 103); and it had become difficult to see the state guaranteeing the ban on Japanese popular culture.

As a result, the moves for cultural decolonization by eliminating Japanese style which had begun immediately after independence were diluted and became isolated. If the primary justification for prohibition was "liquidating" the colonial period, then that justification ought to have collapsed with the failure to "liquidate." Both the Rhee regime, which inherited the governing structures of the colonial period, and Rhee's critics who advocated the liquidation of colonialism, did not strictly adhere to the prohibitions, and thus the ban on Japanese style lost any legitimacy beyond continuing appeals for prohibition.

Japanese style as symbolic of decolonization and modernization

Japanese style as cultural invasion

In the 1960s, especially around the time of the 1965 normalization of diplomatic relations between Japan and Korea, the meaning of Japanese style became more complex. The movement to eliminate Japanese style in the 1950s had been focused on vestiges of colonialism. In the 1960s, when the Korean contemporary media space began to take form, the target shifted to newly permeating Japanese commodities and popular culture. The context for this shift was the rapid growth in consumption of a diverse array of products "Made in Japan" – not only Japanese magazines, novels, songs and so forth, but also foodstuffs such as Aji-no-moto seasoning (MSG) and soya sauce, as well as manufactured goods such as watches, electric fans, cooking stoves, refrigerators, cameras, and televisions (*The Kyunghyang Shinmun* 1960c).

In 1960, when the April 19 Revolution led to Rhee's resignation, the 1950s seemed to have been reduced to memories of war and poverty symbolized by "pork congee" (*kkulkkurijuk*) made from discarded food from U.S. military bases, but it was still a period of extreme poverty, with GDP around US$160 per capita (compared to USA GDP of $3,000 per capita). Under these conditions, people seen wearing Japanese-made shoes and buying Japanese-made goods in department stores, both symbols of modernity, vividly revealed both the extreme economic disparities of the times and differences in class-based perceptions and attitudes to things "made in Japan."

The distribution and consumption of such Japanese goods was made possible by smuggling via Busan Port. Smuggling had been a serious social problem in the 1950s, with things such as clothing, stationery, gemstones, cosmetics, records, pianos, pinball machines and the like flowing in via Korean dealers, naturally, but also through Japanese and U.S. military dealers (*The Chosun Ilbo* 1958).

> Some treacherous smugglers who undermine the nation and its people are importing foreign luxury goods in large quantities. It goes without saying that the dealers' conduct is wrongful, but a foreign-like awakening in our nationals who prefer imported

products and who scorn domestic goods is also necessary. It is truly deplorable that no matter which department stores one visits, there are few domestic goods, and nothing but imported goods on display. According to merchants, Japanese-made contraband sells so well that demand outstrips supply. It is truly deplorable. (*The Kyunghyang Shinmun* 1960a)

In these circumstances, when the military seized government in a coup d'état in 1961 led by Park Chung-hee, the new regime identified smuggling as a prime example of a social trend in need of reformation. With the dual purpose of publicizing the regime's ambitions for an "independent economy" and of converting social dissatisfaction about smuggling into support for the military regime, the new authorities identified smuggling as representative of "past misdeeds," and cracked down on violations while increasing punishments.

In the past, even while compensating for our budget deficit by means of aid from friendly nations, there was a popular tendency among some nationals towards ridiculous luxury and vanity. A mistaken etiquette dictating that wearing foreign-made clothing, using foreign-made cosmetics and smoking foreign-made cigarettes constituted a way of succeeding in life perennially spread and made society chronically diseased. Of course, this was not a malady that involved the entire national population. It was an evil practice controlled by people who swarmed to the cities and made scheming their occupation, as well as evil schools of thought, rotten politicians, and crooked bureaucrats. (*The Dong-A Ilbo* 1961)

Despite this strong rhetoric, though, the Park regime's response to Japanese imports was extremely complicated. Among other things, even while officially banning imports of Japanese culture, the regime remained open to Japanese capital and commodities. To apprehend this fully, we need to understand the political situation and social atmosphere over the several years between the collapse of the Syngman Rhee government due to the April Revolution of 1960 and immediately after the inauguration of the Park Chung-hee military regime.

The April 19 Revolution was a popular protest against the Syngman Rhee government's long years of dictatorial rule, and, according to many of its advocates, was a political turning point – a "liberation" paralleling that of 15 August 1945. It reverberated throughout society, especially as a backlash against various government controls.

This backlash included a rather paradoxical craze for Japanese popular culture, centering on novels. Japanese literary works were translated and published one after another, with newspaper advertisements promoting "Best-sellers that took postwar Japan by storm in one volume" and similar (*The Dong-A Ilbo* 1960c).

As previously mentioned, Syngman Rhee used anti-Japanese nationalism as a means to legitimize his government. However, due to the U.S.'s priorities and total support for Japan in the emerging Cold War order, the extremely pro-American Rhee's anti-Japanese rhetoric was little more than an empty slogan that appealed to nationalist sentiments, but was not accompanied by concrete action. The Japanese literature boom in the early 1960s should be understood as a cultural reaction to the strict censorship and regulation of the Rhee regime, rather than a change in awareness or attitude towards the Other that Japan represented.

Experiences of Japanese popular culture developed even greater complexity when the brief "liberation" that followed the April 19 Revolution came to an end with the establishment of a new military

Image 1.3: A newspaper advertisement for Gomikawa Junpei's book *The Human Condition (Ningen no jōken)* (*The Dong-A Ilbo* 1960c)

regime. On the one hand, anti-Japanese ideology was once again deployed by the new regime, while on the other hand there was a major turn in the Japan–Korea relationship with the 1965 normalization of diplomatic relations.

There was a strange atmosphere in Korean society around 1965. While on the one hand there was increasing resistance to the normalization of Japan–ROK diplomatic relations, all manner of Japanese culture and goods were smuggled in, distributed and consumed. This provoked further criticism, backlash and suchlike, which, in turn, deepened contradictions and conflicts over perceptions and attitudes towards Japan.

The situation was further complicated by the ambiguous attitude of the Park Chung-hee regime. The military regime strove to achieve economic growth by promoting normalization of Japan–ROK diplomatic relations while at the same time seeking to legitimize its government, and was unable to enforce active prohibition measures such as the movement to eliminate Japanese style that the Rhee regime had pursued, even though it invoked anti-Japanese ideology as part of its self-justification. After all, as normalization of diplomatic relations between Japan and Korea meant opening to Japan in a range of domains, the legitimate importation of televisions, radios, and other electronic goods was beginning. Thus, around the time of the 1965 normalization of relations, Japanese popular culture was distinguished from Japanese goods. The ban on Japanese popular culture continued, but with a new contradiction: while it was prohibited for Japanese music to be played via legally-imported "radios, records containing those tunes were smuggled in and freely sold at record shops" (*The JoongAng Ilbo* 1967a). This outcome was born of the irony that popular culture had to be banned to allay public opposition to the normalization of Japan–ROK diplomatic relations.

Under these circumstances, there was mounting fear and dissatisfaction about the inundation by Japanese culture and the government's acquiescence to it, and the anti-Japanese popular culture discourse was reactivated. Many intellectuals, newspapers and magazines, for example, argued that the "expansion of a middle-class cohort" which produced and enjoyed a wholesome Korean culture was urgent, and considered the "inundation by vulgar Japanese culture," "cultural subordination," and "poor cultural taste" to be the most serious issues facing Korean culture at that time (Kim 2007a: 348). Memories of violently-repressive cultural control by the former Japanese empire and anxiety towards a "cultural invasion" by powerful Japanese corporations were major contributors to the ban on Japanese popular culture at the time of the Japan–Korea Basic Treaty.

At the same time, critical discourses around Japanese-style culture arose in a variety of forms. Many intellectuals, especially, developed a discourse on Japanese-style culture in a way that merged negative images of Japan as the Other with a cautious and disdainful gaze towards novel mass media and popular culture. Counter to criticisms of Japanese-style culture in the "liberation space" which treated it as "lingering cultural remnants from the colonial period," the discourse on Japanese-style culture that arose around 1965 mainly criticized a "cultural invasion that permeated after independence through the mass media, and seduced even the young generation that had not experienced colonization" (Shin 1964: 6).

(Re)production of criticism of Japanese-style culture

However, amid a spate of criticism of Japanese-style culture, apprehension towards Japanese capital inflow and criticism of consumerism and hedonism, people's bodies, senses, and desires expressed different priorities than critique in a discursive space (Kim 2007a: 359). Consumption of Japanese newspapers, magazines, and books gradually increased, and the coffee shops and Japanese restaurants that played Japanese popular music became quite common in Seoul. However, it had become increasingly difficult to explain the contradictions and conflicts in practice in terms of the discourse of "eliminating Japanese style" from the "liberation space". The boycott of Japanese products was a typical example.

That boycott of Japanese products, led by university students and citizens' groups, was a critique of the upper class and high-ranking bureaucrats' consumption of Japanese goods, but also of colonial collaborators who maintained power after independence. In the latter case, the boycott was a revolt against the Park Chung-hee regime and its efforts to normalize diplomatic relations with Japan. Whereas the

1950s ban on Japanese style was comparatively rigorously enforced by various government officials, after the April 19 Revolution of 1960, the entities policing the ban became rather ambiguous. That is, the entities which monitored, prosecuted, and censored the trans-bordering of Japanese popular culture had become multilayered and dispersed, rather than remaining confined to government officials.

> In 1965, the Yonsei University Hunger Strike Committee decided to make a "No-buying-Japanese-goods movement" for blocking a Japanese economic invasion into a national movement. The committee denounced the financial conglomerates that had lost their identity as members of the nation and who emulated Japanese enterprises, and the loathsome pro-Japanese faction that was trying to make our country into a market for Japanese products; and, setting up objectives comprising six items, it decided to expand the movement to reject imported luxury items, starting with those made in Japan. (*The Chosun Ilbo* 1965b)

In other words, criticism of Japanese style as an issue of national identity, and the ways in which Japanese popular culture was circulating and being consumed, had become difficult to explain in terms of a unified "Korean" national story. It had become impossible to simply combine the principal discourses in Korean society at the time into a singular consciousness of a "cultural invasion by the former empire." These discourses were: 1) a nationalist discourse that contrasted *waesaek* with "ethnic purity;" 2) a social discourse that problematized the cultural capital attributed to Japanese goods by the more privileged; and 3) a cultural-theoretical discourse that feared the diffusion of "sleazy popular culture."

Moreover, throughout the 1950s, these discourses had both symbolized decolonization, and cracked open the various "discourses on *waesaek*" which had previously been seen as singular. In a situation where memories of the experience of colonization clearly remained strong, the problematization of the permeation of *waesaek* as both "vestiges of former imperialism" and a new "cultural invasion" generated various issues and desires associated with Japanese popular culture that had not been factors in the earlier, quasi-legal ban on Japanese style.

If this is the case, then it is necessary to understand the trans-bordering of Japanese popular culture in Korea in the 1960s as a manifestation of various desires in Korean society interacting in complex ways. When the Japan–Korea Basic Treaty was concluded, the country stood on the brink of a period of high economic growth. At the same time a media culture industry began to form, conveying a modern and prosperous Western-lifestyle via new media and popular culture, much as Japan had enjoyed after its own rapid economic growth. In this context, the Korean desire for Japanese-style culture and Japanese-made goods was characterized by one magazine of the time as being akin to "opium" which arouses desire despite its danger (Shin 1964).

In the political discourse around "prohibition", Japanese popular culture was characterized as a "dangerous visitor" which was forbidden; but in the economic and cultural sites where popular culture operated, an extremely complex gaze and desires were formed through multi-layered projections. This can be primarily attributed to capitalist culture, which valorized symbols of growth and modernization, and strongly affected the base where "trans-bordering" in Korean society always coexisted with the ban on Japanese popular culture.

Japanese style as a means of rule and mobilization

The Park Chung-hee regime and Japanese style

For Park's military regime, which was compelled to achieve strong economic growth to legitimize itself, the normalization of diplomatic relations with Japan was a vital turning point that enabled the mobilization of development capital from Japan. However, at the same time, it displaced political and cultural decolonization as its first priority, and thus threatened the regime's legitimacy (Kim 1999: 159; Takasaki 1996: 185). The regime's ambiguous stance on culture, and especially popular culture, was arguably assumed cognizant of this dilemma.

Of course, for a time immediately after the normalization of diplomatic relations, the Park regime was positively disposed towards the Japan–Korea cultural relationship, such as importing and screening Japanese films (The Ministry of Culture and Sports of South Korea 1978). However, the Korean government's policy of permitting the importation of Japanese films met fierce resistance from the public. Considering that social perceptions around Japanese popular culture had been gradually softening since the April 19 Revolution of 1960, this backlash clearly signified opposition to the normalization of Japan–ROK diplomatic relations. Ultimately, the Park regime, burdened by a public perception that it was a "pro-Japanese government,"[2] revoked that policy and prohibited the importation of Japanese films (*JoongAng Ilbo* 1966c). From this point on, rather than the ban on Japanese popular culture being simply government policy, it was legitimized by the complex of perceptions and sentiments in Korean society.

> The government's considering cultural exchange, including ex-change of cultural personnel between Korea and Japan and do-mestic screening of Japanese films, is a disgraceful act that again displays … the current government's undue emphasis on Japan to which it was subordinated as a whole, encompassing political, economic, and cultural fields. (*The JoongAng Ilbo* 1967b)

As this critique implies, Park Chung-hee, a graduate of the Manchurian Army Academy and former Second Lieutenant in the Eighth Company of the Manchurian Army Infantry via the Imperial Japanese Army Academy in the colonial period (Kang and Hyun 2010: 16), was per-

---

2   The *Asahi Shinbun* explains the meaning of the pro-Japanese faction as follows: The way of calling people members of the "pro-Japanese faction" (Chinilpa in Korean) was also used to refer to Koreans who cooperated with Japanese authorities under colonial domination in the past, not in the present day. In the Republic of Korea, a bad image accompanies this no-menclature, signifying "having betrayed the [Korean] ethnos" (*The Asahi Shinbun* 2001). In other words, in Korea, the expression "pro-Japanese" has a completely different meaning from the "pro-Japanese" used in Japan. For that reason, in this book I have used the expression "colonial collaborators", which is closer to its original sense, rather than "pro-Japanese", but in the case of "pro-Japanese regime", I will spell it as is, because it is a fixed term used in relation to the Park government.

ceived to harbor lingering affection for Japan. In contrast to how post-independence Korean society's general desires were directed towards the U.S., Park's life and values seemed to focus on "Japanese-like modernization." In fact, the greater part of the "Fatherland modernization" policy Park advocated was modelled on the Japanese modernization process (Kang 2004: 125).

> President Park was excessively fond of westerns and samurai films... In those days, when the importation of Japanese films was taboo, as it is now, one of the important duties of personnel from the Korean Central Intelligence Agency (KCIA) who were stationed in Japan was to choose films worth watching and sending them via diplomatic pouch to Cheong Wa Dae. Mr C., a former KCIA executive, recalls: "When I was working in Japan, I used to collect almost all samurai films, as well as films and television dramas set around the time of the Meiji Restoration, and send them to the home country"... And President Park's son states: "My father used to watch them just once a year, in the summer vacation, at our holiday house". (*The JoongAng Ilbo* 1992b)

The military regime that was perceived to be pro-Japanese continued to emphasize "national democracy," "national revival," "Korean democracy," "national identity," an "independent economy," "autonomous national defense," "citizenship education" and similar in reference to the nation and its people throughout its lengthy term of government (1961–1979). Through "developmentalist mobilization" and "anti-communist mobilization", it sought national approval for its policies (Cho 2010: 249).

   Nationalism was, in many respects, contradicted by the historical condition of being a "divided country" and its anti-communist ideology. However, the Park regime legitimized its government with a discourse of "fatherland modernization," and actively deployed nationalist rhetoric for training and mobilizing members of the nation. In short, the dictatorship used nationalism to justify the wide range of developmental policies, including the normalization of Japan–ROK diplomatic relations (Jeon 1998: 89).

"A Camellia of a Girl" and the prohibition of *waesaek* tunes

From the beginning of the Park regime, *waesaek* not only specified Japanese popular culture, but was employed as a means of controlling Korean domestic popular culture. As it became increasingly difficult to control cultural flows across its borders, a "border reversal" was implemented which directed censorship internally.

The representative target was songs. Around the time of the Basic Treaty and normalization of diplomatic relations, the military regime heavy-handedly suppressed civil resistance by political and cultural regulations (Yoo 1999: 47). Deliberations on "music broadcasting" by the newly established Advisory Committee on Songs began in 1965, when the Basic Treaty was ratified, illustrating such suppression in the cultural domain (Moon 2004: 17–18). Thereafter, the ban on Japanese style was used as a means of political censorship.

According to a list of banned songs published in 1981 by the Broadcasting Deliberation Committee, a total of 787 domestic tunes were banned from airplay over sixteen years, from March 1965 until September 1981. Of those, 296 tunes were banned from broadcast for reasons related to Japanese style, including Japanese recordings (247 songs), plagiarism of Japanese tunes (46 songs), plagiarism of Japanese-style or Japanese melodies (2 songs), and Japanese-language songs (1 song).

Banning "A Camellia of a Girl" (published in 1964) especially shocked the country. This song, which describes a woman's spite and sorrow, was sung by one of post-independence Korea's most famous singers, Lee Mija, and boasted unprecedented popularity; but just as its popularity reached its peak, it was banned due to its Japanese style. This incident indicates that Japanese style was exploited not only as a means of cultural politics, but also as political censorship. As public objections to the Basic Treaty increased in ferocity, the government "strove to emphasize the point that they themselves were nationals by ostentatiously slapping the label of *waesaek* [onto the most popular music at the time] and banning it" (Lee 1998: 177). Popular music critic Lee Youngmi further states as follows:

The reason for banning "A Camellia of a Girl" was that it smelt of a "Japanese-style song", but having banned those tunes due to their seeming to be *waesaek* represents the pinnacle of paradox for Park Chung-hee, who loved Japanese things more than anyone, having graduated from the Imperial Japanese Army Academy and who enjoyed Japanese samurai films at his [official residence,] Cheong Wa Dae. On the other hand, one theory that says Park Chung-hee continued fondly to sing "A Camellia of a Girl" simply expresses this comedic duality. (Lee 2002: 136)

In other words, the ban on "A Camellia of a Girl" at the time can be understood as an example of "symbolic manipulation" conducted to redress the "pro-Japanese" image that dogged the regime, while at the same time suppressing opposition to the normalization of Japan–ROK diplomatic relations (*The Hankyoreh* 2005). This was probably possible because practices around Japanese style were widely shared in the community (Steiner 1956), as the structural contradictions surrounding decolonization had begun to be internalized as a "rule" in Korean popular culture.

Among the more obvious of these structural contradictions was the fact that the very Japanese popular culture that was supposedly banned was being widely consumed even as domestic music was being censored for emulating Japanese style. After all, it was the general public's desire for Japanese popular culture that made it the target of legal prohibition. However, any moral or rational justification for legal prohibition of desire is substantively undermined within a process that, on the one hand, censors domestic producers for vague reasons of style, while tacitly approving the steady influx of Japanese popular culture. The legal prohibition of Japanese popular culture was not only ineffective, but counter-productive. The question of what comprises *waesaek*, or what is an appropriate object for prohibition, is not important: rather, the Park regime's efforts to develop a Korean popular culture by censoring and suppressing domestic consumption of Japanese style popular culture served instead to reinforce Korean desire and demand for Japanese style.

This example, in particular, sheds light on the nature of the ban on Japanese popular culture as a historical construct, illustrating that the ban initiated in the 1950s as a regulator of domestic popular culture – meant to contribute to the task of decolonization in the "liberation space" – began from the mid-1960s to assume the character of a prohibition by the same type of political censorship that had fettered colonial Korea and the post-independence Republic of Korea throughout the era of American military government.

Chapter 2

THE INTERSECTION OF THE U.S. AND THE BAN

The social motivation for the "ban on Japanese popular culture" – decolonization – conflicted with and contradicted the drive for modernization, which was a greater motivator. At its core was the overwhelming power called "America," which linked Japan and Korea.

American hegemony and the Cold-War cultural map

A Cold-War-like cultural formation in the "liberation space"

The most important "bordering" factor and actor in the new Republic of Korea was "America." The issue of prohibitions on imported cultural products can only be properly understood in terms of the emerging "Cold War structure" and the irresistible power of the absolute Other that was America. Korea's decolonization and modernization firmly suppressed popular culture and everyday consciousness, while anti-communism and pro-Americanism were entangled with the potent ideology of a developmental dictatorship. In short, to understand the "ban on Japanese popular culture," we must examine the various "oppressions" that shaped postcolonial Korean society.

At the moment of liberation in 1945, the enormous political and cultural influence that Japan had exercised in Korean society moved almost immediately to the United States, with the rapidly forming Cold War system accelerating that change. Korea was the site of the

U.S. military's first efforts at containment vis-à-vis the Soviet Union and communism (Cumings 1981). Accordingly, the newly liberated Korea's ambitions to break away from Japanese influence were almost immediately subordinated to the process of creating a new state system closely allied with surrounding countries in the form of the Cold War order.

The first stage of creating a new state system occurred during the period of U.S. military administration, from 1945 until 1948. From immediately after its 1945 independence, rulings concerning the mechanisms of law and order, including the Korean Department of Justice, the courts, and national police were handed down mainly by the U.S. military. The initial "Koreanization" after liberation was not the work of Korean nationals, but instead was directed by the U.S. military. However, this "Koreanization" was nothing more than a procedure for transferring the judicial organs created by the Japanese colonizers to the Koreans, unaltered. The personnel and organizational structures were inherited intact, and until the end of the U.S. occupation, there were no substantial structural changes, including in the treatment of Korean staff who had collaborated with the colonizers.

The national "border" that post-independence Korean society strove to construct was built according to the Cold War order imposed by the military, political, and ideological standards of the U.S. military administration. The U.S. applied the same standards to Japanese popular culture, which in Korea was the principal target of decolonization. But in policy vis-à-vis Japan, Cold War strategies were a higher priority than decolonization. As a "cultural vestige" of colonial rule, trans-bordering by Japanese popular culture was perceived as a "cultural invasion" by those focused on decolonization, while at the same time being perceived as modernization in the context of the Cold-War strategy. In other words, while Japanese popular culture was on the one hand perceived as a source of fear and insecurity, on the other hand that culture offered the modernization necessary for defeating North Korea in a global competition, and for drawing closer to the U.S.

Accordingly, to understand the nature of the cultural border with Japan which Korean society constructed through the discourses of a "ban", it is necessary to examine not only the relationship between Japan and Korea as former colonizer and colonized, but also the relationship with the border that was created between the U.S. and North Korea in the Cold War structure. For several decades, the cultural relationship between Japan and Korea was fluid and multilayered, in a situation where decolonization, modernization, the Cold War, as well as various conditions of "developmentalism" imposed by the dictatorship, operated in complex ways.

U.S. military rule and the media order

The U.S. military administration governing Korea implemented censorship and prohibitions targeting diverse media, including films, broadcasting, newspapers, and magazines. A stringent legal system was established based upon American ideals and values.

Through its 1946 Film ordinance, the United States Army Military Government in Korea (USAMGIK)'s OCI (Office of Civil Information) endeavored to curb the production of leftist films and at the same time propagate U.S.-style democracy. The criterion for censorship of a film lay in whether it was injurious to democracy or USAMGIK. Before a film could be shown it had to get permission from the OCI or be treated as illegal. The censorship criteria became a model for film production, and the subject matter and themes that Korean films explored were limited to those permitted by the U.S. military (Yeom 2008: 443–445).

USAMGIK also intervened directly in newspaper and magazine publishing, forcibly closing those aligned with the Communist Party and those advocating for a more progressive democracy. This aggressive regulation of speech continued after June 1947, when it allowed the "South Korean Interim Government" to form, while retaining the north-south division (Kim 1995: 14–16). A broad array of propaganda activities was conducted throughout this period. OCI's vigorous anti-communist and anti-North Korea propaganda activities included the production of 315 tons of publications, distributed through 65 different magazines and 7.7 million copies, as well as the publication of seventy issues of *Segye sinbo* totaling 8.3 million copies (Kim 2011: 82). In other words, the "cultural Cold War" waged in South Korea comprised two pillars: extensive regulation and censorship, and proactive propaganda activities, which combined to consolidate America's politico-economic and socio-cultural influence.

This cultural relationship with the U.S. was built upon a Cold-War cultural map. Total reliance on the U.S. went hand-in-hand with military confrontation and ideological competition with North Korea. North Korea and communism were identified as enemies which had to be thoroughly excluded. This attitude manifested in the media space as a stringent censorship regime targeting North Korea and communism, which would be reproduced and strengthened after the government of the Republic of Korea was established in 1948 (Yeom 2008: 446). Through the Korean War (1950–53), especially, anti-communist regulations and sentiments became both deeply-rooted and far-reaching, extending beyond the legal system and into the hearts and minds of the people, becoming a powerful and dominant ideology.

The point is that with post-independence Korean culture so strongly shaped by a clear-cut cultural map defined by friends (the U.S.) and foes (North Korea) (Lee 2008a: 11), the rather ambiguous cultural border with Japan was extremely complicated and cannot be adequately explained in terms of anti-Japanese nationalism. It was formed in a shared historical context, but it was also unprecedented, generated by new geopolitical conditions.

The further the U.S. infiltrated the border, and the deeper South Korea engaged in competition with North Korea, the more important Japan became as an Other that could not be excluded. If we accept that the U.S. was so influential that it substantially shaped Korea's media space, it is not difficult to likewise accept that it was necessary to build a close political and economic relationship with Japan, one of the U.S.'s closest allies in the region, thus setting aside or at least undermining efforts at decolonization.

Internal cultural trans-bordering from USAMGIK bases

The formation of American media and urban space

In circumstances where almost all aspects of political, economic and social life in Korean society were determined by security considerations (Moon 1997), "American things" became hegemonic, progressively penetrating Korean popular culture and everyday consciousness. Democracy and liberalism from the U.S. were embraced as unquestionable ideals, and American culture permeated the capital, Seoul, and throughout the country, centered upon U.S. military bases. Such elements as U.S. military broadcasts (AFKN), troop entertainment by the Eighth Army, and a black market for goods from the U.S. military retail store known as "PX" (Post Exchange) built a new media and urban space. The Korean experience closely paralleled postwar Japan's, which was directly governed by the U.S. GHQ as an overwhelming occupying power from 1945 to 1952 (Yoshimi 2002: 23).

In the period of U.S. military administration and throughout the Korean War, the U.S. was perceived as a land of plenty, providing not only food and clothing, but also a variety of machinery and equipment. The large inflow of "things" via the U.S. military created a concrete image of America – one that made no class distinction. For most Koreans, from the poor who relied on the U.S. military's consumer behavior to the ruling class who accepted that studying in the U.S. was necessary for success in life,[1] America was the very model of civilization.

The capital, Seoul, was recast as an urban space that displayed and consumed America itself, and Hollywood films became a media space for experiencing the modern age that was America (Lee 2006: 76–78). Korean audiences, who were depoliticized and suppressed by strict prohibitions and exclusion vis-à-vis communism and North Korea, responded to this new urban and media space with a strong and growing desire for further Americanization (Yeom 2008: 449).

The extent of the effects on Korean popular culture was in no small part due to the economic influences of the U.S. military units. For example, Korean bars, clubs, cabaret and theaters catering to the U.S. military personnel flourished (Aoki 2013), as they did in Japan. The Korean musicians and managers who worked at those facilities reportedly earned up to one million dollars per year, more than the total Korean export earnings at the time. The Korean economy was

---

1   Korean universities, like many institutions, directly imitated their U.S. counterparts during the post-independence period, and the experience of studying in America became an established part of intellectual/elite culture, further contributing to the Americanization of Korean society (Lee 2009b: 238–239).

suffering from inflation, and the entertainment industry serving the U.S. military was a crucial source of dollars (Shin and Ho 2008: 348).

One product of this situation was the growth of a systematic entertainment management industry comprised of a number of major entertainment agencies. Shin Jung-hyun, who hailed from the so-called "Eighth Army Band" and is now considered to be Korea's legendary guitarist, recounts as follows:

> At the time, the Eighth Army Band required [aspiring members] to audition in front of American entertainment specialists every six months... In those days, major entertainment agencies like "Hua-yang", "20th Century" and "Universal" supplied entertainers to the U.S. military stage. Each agency led more than twenty show groups and bands. A show group was a team in which a variety of artists, such as dancers and singers, comedians and magicians were combined with a band, while a band was a team that only played music. (Shin 2006: 77–78)

Importantly, it was not only cultural products in circulation. In circumstances where material aid from the U.S. military was an important source of goods, American products and everyday culture dominated consumer culture in the cities, further spreading the popular culture mediated by U.S. military units.

The permeation of foreign culture and goods through the U.S. military restructured the Korean people's very lifestyle (Lee 2009b: 237–238). The lifestyle of the colonial period was dismantled and reconstructed to fit a frame produced by the new world system (Kim 2007b: 312). The modern Korean culture of the colonial period was a replication of a Westernized modern Japanese lifestyle, and the new popular culture of the Cold War directly imitated an American lifestyle (Lee 2008b: 394). In other words, the "de-Japanization" of Korea was not merely a process of "decolonization," but entailed a political and cultural assimilation with the U.S., effectively transforming East Asia "from a Japanese Empire to an American Empire" (Jeong 2009).

The AFKN (American Forces Korea Network; AFN Korea from 2001), whose main purpose was to provide a broadcasting service to the U.S. military, symbolically expressed the American-style media space, urban space, and everyday life. The AFKN effect was ostensibly "spillover" from its primary audience on U.S. military bases, while simultaneously functioning as domestic terrestrial broadcast signals.

Naturally, the latest popular music and films from the U.S. were actively promoted by the AFKN. Just as the distribution of American goods such as tobacco, whisky, coffee, Coca-Cola and so forth through the PX significantly reconfigured the Korean urban space and consumption lifestyle, AFKN TV was the main medium through which ordinary people encountered advanced popular culture from foreign countries. That is to say, while anti-communism and anti-Japanese sentiments underpinned South Korean national identity, the U.S. was the primary source of permitted cultural contact. Various cultural products that became available via AFKN television broadcasts, Hollywood movies, and the PX were not merely consumer objects, but also symbolized the modernization that ought to be aspired to. Under the circumstances, American culture was not merely a foreign culture that had entered the country. Rather, it was fundamental and foundational in the formation of the Korean media and popular culture industries; indeed, it was the most potent influence on Korean

Image 2.1: American film advertisements carried in a newspaper at the time (*The Kyunghyang Shinmun* 1960b)

culture, enhanced with a policy of strict exclusion of North Korean and communist bloc culture.

The post-independence relationship with Japan was constructed in accordance with this Cold-War cultural map. In which case, it would be impossible to explain the cultural relationship between Japan and Korea solely in terms of a "Japan–Korea" frame, or to understand the continuing consumption of Japanese popular culture as a simple expression of desire for the former empire. The more inviolable construct of the "Cold War" and the more massive U.S. empire provided the background of the Japan–Korea relationship. Moreover, the Japan–Korea relationship was a crucial factor in America's Cold War strategy: in other words, for postwar Japan and Korea, which harbored all manner of mutual animosity arising from their colonial experience, the U.S. functioned as a medium for overcoming that animosity.

The intersection of the Cold War media space and Japanese culture

Contradictions and discord over the "ban-worthy Other"

As previously mentioned, the ban on Japanese popular culture changed in a completely different way from the legal ban on North Korea and communist culture. Although various measures to erase remnants of colonial rule were taken throughout the country immediately following independence on the government's initiative, anti-Japanese movements never took the form of a complete blockade, as there was against communism, nor was there a legal prohibition, such as the Anti-communist Law and National Security Act.

The difference was probably inevitable, considering the historical and geopolitical conditions of the Cold War. For example, Syngman Rhee, who, despite having been an independence activist, retained in his government the colonial collaborators whom the USAMGIK had appointed to senior bureaucratic posts, and Park Chung-hee, who had served in the Japanese Imperial Army, anti-Japanese nationalism was a necessary ideology for assuring the legitimacy of their own administrations, rather than something crucial to establishing a national identity. However, although both "anti-Japanese" and "anti-communism" were valid ideologies for the sake of governance, bans enacted due to anti-Japanese policy were not policed by powerful censors such as USAMGIK which enforced bans against communism.

Among other things, anti-communism and anti-Japanese were fundamentally contradictory positions. The principal U.S. Cold War strategy in East Asia was to create a structure of security and economic cooperation with Japan as its "core state" (Katzenstein 2005), and to locate South Korea and Taiwan within it. Under this system, Japan's influence on Korea was not a relic of the past that had ended with independence, but a strong and continuous presence. Beyond the specific challenge of "liquidating the remains of the Japanese Empire", which was part of USAMGIK's propaganda policy in South Korea, the Japan–Korea relationship was a vital axis in the U.S. strategy towards Asia. Furthermore, considering Korea's dependence on the Japanese economy in its ambitions to modernize, it was always necessary to maintain a tightly knit political and economic relationship.

Hence, at the precise moment when decolonization had begun, the cultural border with Japan began to be reconstituted in complex and ambiguous ways. As such, the ban on Japanese popular culture operated vaguely in a quasi-legal form that relied upon discourse in the absence of concrete laws and policies, in contrast to the stringent regulation, censorship, et cetera, vis-à-vis North Korea and communist culture.

Nevertheless, the normalization of diplomatic relations between Japan and the Republic of Korea discussed in Chapter One constituted an important turning point. Diplomatic relations between Japan and Korea were established on June 22, 1965, with the signing of numerous agreements based on the Treaty on Basic Relations between Japan and the Republic of Korea.[2] As stipulated also in the *White Paper on*

---

2 These included the Agreement between Japan and the Republic of Korea Concerning the Settlement of Problems in Regard to Property and Claims and Economic Cooperation; the Agreement between Japan and the Republic of Korea Concerning Fisheries; the Agreement between Japan and the Republic of Korea Concerning the Legal Status and Treatment of the People of the Republic of Korea Residing in Japan; and the Agreement between Japan and the Republic of Korea Concerning Cultural Properties and Cultural Cooperation.

Talks between the Republic of Korea and Japan, these agreements prioritized the U.S. Far East strategy and the political aims of the Korean government, and were pushed through despite a variety of unresolved issues concerning territory, history and suchlike, and against vehement domestic opposition. The government's reasoning is explained in the following statement:

> It is an undeniable fact that the normalization of diplomatic relations between the Republic of Korea and Japan will strengthen the solidarity of the trilateral relationship between Korea, the United States and Japan, promote international relationships of economic cooperation, and, in terms of the state, become the basis for achieving the establishment of a free economic system and economic prosperity for victory over communism and for unification. (The Government of the Republic of Korea 1965: 148)

After the normalization of diplomatic relations, Japan and Korea were increasingly engaged in exchange-relations, not only economically, but in all fields. When one considers that bolstering the legitimacy of the regime through economic development using Japanese capital was crucial for the Park administration, it is clear that efforts to exclude Japanese popular culture were exceptional in the Japan–Korea relationship.

The effective absence of content relating to "cultural cooperation" apart from cultural properties in the 1965 Agreement between Japan and the Republic of Korea Concerning Cultural Properties and Cultural Cooperation symbolically attests to that situation.

"Agreement between Japan and the Republic of Korea concerning Cultural Assets and Cultural Cooperation" (June 22, 1965)[3]

---

3 "Agreement between Japan and the Republic of Korea Concerning Cultural Properties and Cultural Cooperation", based on the "Treaty on Basic Relations between Japan and the Republic of Korea", signed at Tokyo on 22 June 1965; *Basic Documents on Japanese Foreign Relations*, Vol. 2, 600–601; Ministry of Foreign Affairs Treaty Division "Treaty Compilation (Bilateral Treaty)" database; "The World and Japan" Japanese political and international relations database, cited from Tanaka Akihiko Research Office, Institute for Advanced Studies on Asia, The University of Tokyo (https://worldjpn.grips.ac.jp/documents/index.html).

Japan and the Republic of Korea

Considering the historical cultural relations between their two countries;

And

Hoping to contribute to the development and studies of their sciences and culture,

Have agreed as follows:

Article I
The Government of Japan and the Government of the Republic of Korea shall render the fullest possible Cooperation in order to promote cultural relations between the peoples of the two countries.

Article II
The Government of Japan shall, in accordance with the procedures agreed upon between the Governments of the two countries, transfer to the Government of the Republic of Korea the cultural assets listed in the Annex within six months of the date on which the present Agreement enters into force.

Article III
The Government of Japan and the Government of the Republic of Korea shall accord each other with every possible facility to provide the nationals of the other country with the opportunities to study the cultural assets possessed by art museums, museums, libraries, and other facilities of science and culture of its country.

The "Korea–Japan Cultural Exchange Plan" sent internally from the Ministry of Culture and Sports to the Minister of Foreign Affairs indicates that the Park regime was fully aware of the nature of the "Cultural Agreement."

1. At this time the "Agreement between the Republic of Korea and Japan concerning Cultural Assets and Cultural Cooperation" (Treaty no. 181) and "Record of Agreement Proceedings" (Treaty no. 182) based on the Korea–Japan Basic Treaty have been ratified and have come into effect.

2. *The abovementioned two treaties make the matter of the return of cultural properties their subject; and cannot be said to be "cultural agreements" concluded with the government of another country.*

3. Japan desires the conclusion of a cultural agreement, but, in consideration of the structural fragility of our culture and the anti-Japanese sentiments of the people, the conclusion of an agreement has been delayed due to the position of conducting exchange incrementally, starting from pure art. (The Ministry of Culture and Sports of South Korea 1978, emphasis added)

In addition, according to materials held by the Embassy of the Republic of Korea in Japan entitled "Korea–Japan Cultural Exchange" composed in December 1979, the Japan–Korea relationship and exchange in the cultural domain were hardly ever discussed at a government level, beyond mentions at the Japan–Korea Cabinet Ministers' Meetings in the late 1960s and early 1970s, and Japan–Korea Parliamentarians' Fellowship gatherings. As such, in both Japan and Korea, which shared the aims of maintaining the Cold War system and high economic growth, questions of the "cultural domain" were formally left "absent" even after the normalization of diplomatic relations.

However, this does not mean that all cultural exchange with Japan was denied, as demonstrated in Article I of the "Agreement between Japan and the Republic of Korea concerning Cultural Assets and Cultural Cooperation" which states: "The Government of Japan and the Government of the Republic of Korea shall render the fullest possible Cooperation in order to promote cultural relations between the peoples of the two countries." In an atmosphere in which culture was understood in terms of so-called "high culture" and "popular culture," and where the popularity of jazz and popular music was feared, while the spread of opera was perceived as cultural progress for Korea (*The Dong-A Ilbo* 1965), "popular culture" was deemed to be problematic. While on the one hand "the expansion of exchange in the fields of high-class culture, science and technology, and education [were] welcomed" (*The Dong-A Ilbo* 1968), popular culture such as films and popular songs, comics and popular novels was singled out as being harmful to national identity. Such a social gaze vis-a-vis popular culture was arguably central to the later ban on Japanese popular culture.

Capitalist culture and Japanese style

As discussed, Korean popular culture and everyday consciousness in the 1960s was formed amid the intersection and clash of opposing mechanisms of modern oppression: decolonization and the Cold War structure. While retaining traces of Japanization inscribed on their bodies, the Korean public simultaneously displayed a strong desire to be Americanized under USAMGIK after the Korean War (Lee 2008b: 388). The affluent Western lifestyle that Japan had begun to enjoy through high economic growth provided a more tangible model for pursuing the aspirations to emulate the U.S. on the level of everyday life. If America were just too distant a presence for the realization of that aspiration, however fervently desired, then the system for consuming "America" that spread in Japan from the 1950s onwards (Yoshimi 2002: 58) offered a substantial model that could be taken as a reference and copied (Kim 2007a: 357). The desire, gaze and strategy relating to American and Japanese "things" were progressively absorbed without modification into the Cold War cultural space. In a cultural space where censorship and discipline imposed anti-communism and liberal democracy, suppressing popular culture and everyday consciousness, Japanese popular culture was always desired and enjoyed alongside American things. In this cultural space, Japan was a Cold War ally, not a former colonizer, and Japanese popular culture was not perceived as cultural imperialism to be rejected, but a model for modernization worthy of imitation in order to draw nearer to the U.S. standard of living, as postwar Japan had done.

In other words, the prohibition of Japanese popular culture, which was the major challenge in the de-colonized cultural space, was neither a priority in the Cold War cultural space, nor a criterion capable of being observed. The only things permitted within the overwhelming forces of Americanization were the desires, gazes and strategies subordinate to the order of the Cold War system.

Accordingly, in Korea, which touted economic growth and modernization as the most important tasks for the state, rigidly excluding Japanese popular culture by means of legal prohibition contradicted the trajectory of media-space formation.

After all, since a market handling Japanese products was long-established, it was impossible to specifically ban popular culture, because Japanese products, including popular culture, had always been actively consumed through that market. Much of these imports were via the black market. All kinds of products, including clothing, stationery, gemstones, cosmetics, records, calculators, high-class scarves, watches and televisions, were brought in by U.S. military PXs and smuggling vessels. However, alternatively, products made in Japan were also sometimes openly displayed in department stores and the like (*The Chosun Ilbo* 1960). Stalls selling Japanese newspapers, magazines, and so forth, and coffee shops where Japanese songs were played, rapidly came to be typical in everyday urban spaces, to the extent that people forgot the movement to get rid of Japanese style from the liberation space (*The Dong-A Ilbo* 1960b). As the U.S. began integrating the former Japanese colonies into a regional trading network centered on Japan (Arrighi 1994: 353), Japanese popular culture came to represent a form of capitalist culture.

The absence of a system legally regulating the culture industry directly manifested as the absence of a legal system governing the influx of Japanese popular culture. Thus, although there was broad social discourse that was critical and fearful of the "massive spread of Japanese culture in the various fields of literature, cinema, music, broadcasting, and so on, and in food, clothing and shelter generally" (*The Chosun Ilbo* 1965a), means for stringently regulating Japanese popular culture were effectively absent, as can be seen in the fact that advertisements for Japanese products were still carried in the local newspapers, for example. In 1960s South Korea, where the capitalist market remained rather feeble, the presence of Japanese advertisements was seen as symbolizing new market exploitation by Japanese industry, with its large-scale production and consumption patterns (Choi 1963). Amid the heightened desire for economic development, Japanese style was transformed from a simple vestige of colonialism into a representation of capitalist culture, which was both feared and longed for.

This cultural relationship with Japan had a significant impact on the structure of the Korean media industry, which thoroughly depended upon systems introduced from the U.S. Thus, while it was being vigorously cultivated under a state-led developmentalist logic, technical and material installations from Japan were essential, along with U.S. influence.

The state, which had not formulated any substantial administrative system to deal with the inflow of Japanese popular culture, displayed a different attitude in the 1960s to that in the 1950s. The position of the government, which had welcomed the normalization of diplomatic relations at the time, was ambiguous – neither forward-looking nor tacitly approving: the Head of the Department of Public Information stated that "if things are fair and rational, then even if they are from Japan, we should accept them, but sleazy Japanese things should be especially rejected" (*The Dong-A Ilbo* 1964a); while the national parliament emphasized the removal of *waesaek* rather than a total ban (National Assembly of the Republic of Korea 1961).

In those circumstances, the influx of Japanese popular media expanded markedly. According to the first nationwide public opinion poll on broadcasting conducted by the Office of Public Information's Broadcasting Control Bureau, Japanese radio broadcasts accounted for 7.3% of the listening audience in 1960, when there was a total of 780,000 radio sets in Korea. This was a considerably higher market share than AFKN at 3.9%, and the Voice of America (VOA) at 2.3% (*The Dong-A Ilbo* 1960a).

In cinema, too, the Japanese influence was extreme. Although Hollywood movies dominated the 1950s Korean cinema market, 80% of them were imported via Japan through an Asian market expansion strategy by the U.S. film industry. Among distributors, the leader was Japan's Fuji Trading Film Division. Fuji Trading was an important supply route from the Japanese cinema community to Korea, sending the Japanese cinema periodical, *Kinema Junpō*, and Japanese advertising flyers and posters to Korean businesspeople and bureaucrats in charge of film. Hence, most information about cinema at the time came from an unadulterated Japanese perspective (Lee 2010: 93–94).

The realm in which Japan exerted the greatest influence, alongside America, was television broadcasting (Cho 2008; Lim 2004). First, the formal beginning of television broadcasting with the launch of the KBS (Korean Broadcasting System) station promoted by the Park regime when it came to power was based on the importation of 20,000 television sets from Japan (*The Kyunghyang Shinmun* 1961). As television broadcasting was hurriedly launched for the sake of the military regime's political interests, the Korean television broadcasting system was extremely poor. Software, especially, that is, the format and content of programs, was influenced by Japan in various ways. After TBCTV (Tongyang Broadcasting Company TV) launched in 1964, equipped with portable VTRs (Video Tape Recorders), it began to copy the format of successful Japanese television dramas. In those days, Japan's television broadcasting system was an important site of learning, to the extent that one course available for Korean producers was production-process training at NHK, TBS, Nippon Television and others in Japan.

Moreover, children's programming was highly dependent upon Japanese programs, too. The Japanese animated cartoon, *Kaitei shōnen Marin*, for instance, was broadcast to launch MBCTV, titled "Marine Boy" (The 30-year History of Munhwa Broadcasting Corporation

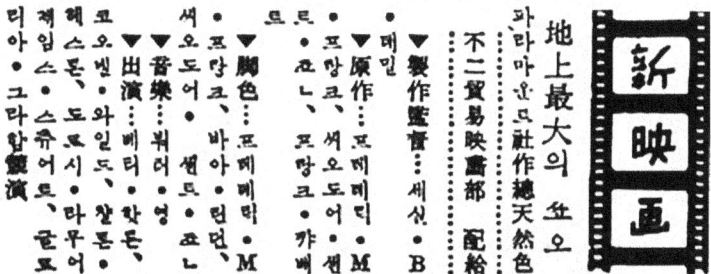

Image 2.2: An article introducing ""The Greatest Show on Earth" distributed by the "Fuji Trading Film Division" (*The Dong-A Ilbo* 1955)

Committee 1992: 739). In short, Japanese television broadcasting was a supplier of both hardware and software, as well as an object of learning and imitation in Korean broadcast production.

Interlacing the American and Japanese

In those circumstances, the issue of Japanese style had become something which the Korean culture industry and policy system could not respond to effectively, because all kinds of Japanese cultural content had to be routed through the American media.

A typical example demonstrating the complexity of the issue of Japanese style was the 1962 Korean screening of the film, *The Teahouse of the August Moon*, produced by MGM in the U.S. in 1956 and released in Japan in 1957. Set in Okinawa and depicting the story of an American soldier and a Japanese geisha, it was rejected by the Rhee administration's Nationwide Committee for Film Ethics due to its dense Japanese style, but was nevertheless recommended for importation, which had huge repercussions for the Korean film industry.

The film industry protested the Department of Public Information's (an administrative body in charge of operations analogous to Japan's

Image 2.3:
A poster for The Teahouse of the August Moon hung at Daehan Theatre
(*The Kyunghyang Shinmun* 1962b)

Agency for Cultural Affairs) recommendation of importation because of "the potential for the domestic screening of Japanese-style films and the resulting atrophy of domestically-produced cinema" (*The Kyunghyang Shinmun* 1962b). Designed in 1956 by 20th Century Fox in the U.S., the 1900-seat Daehan Theatre where the screening was scheduled was the largest cinema in Korea at the time. The exhibition of a film that positively depicted Japanese customs – in short, Japanese style – in such a venue symbolically repudiated the previous policy vis-à-vis Japanese style.

This event represented a dilemma of Japanese style.[4] After it was recommended for importation, a violent confrontation between domestic filmmakers and the foreign film industry over screening permission embarrassed the government. Even though certain works were labeled *waesaek*, there was no legal apparatus to control their importation if they were made in the USA. With difficulty, the Department of Public Information decided to respond "on a case-by-case basis, according to the content of each" film, but the cinema community rejected this as a "trade-off" (*The Dong-A Ilbo* 1963a).

After *The Teahouse of the August Moon* was formally granted screening permission in August 1963, the importation of American films and the production of domestic films depicting Japanese customs increased. This meant that Japanese style had become troublesome and had to continue to be banned in a situation where it was legally unenforceable. The sight of kimono-clad Japanese actress Kyō Machiko pictured on the Daehan Theatre's huge billboard caused considerable shock and confusion to Korean society. Faced with Japanese style imported as capitalist culture, Korean society began to realize that a new order was imminent and they could not respond solely with the sentiments of a colonized people. In the culture industry, the issue of Japanese style was dealt with not by simple prohibition and contravention, but in a more complex and ambiguous way, which came to characterize the Korean popular culture industry.

AFKN, too, was a major route for the inflow of Japanese popular culture. Japanese films and anime that were banned from domestic

---

4   The Department of Public Information had "plunged into a dilemma" (*The Dong-A Ilbo* 1962).

broadcasts were aired via AFKN. There was never any South Korean government regulation of that practice, because, as the newspaper article below states in regard to American broadcasts originally aimed at serving the U.S. military, it was impossible for the Korean government to exercise control over programming on the pretext of its own relations with Japan.

> Already, several films whose importation was forbidden in our country due to their excessively sexual depiction had already been shown in AFKN's late-night broadcasts, and in summer, the Japanese film, *Rashomon*, was also aired. We cannot make an issue of that programming because it is television meant for U.S. troops stationed in Korea. It is necessary for guardians to keep this situation in mind, and have the intelligence to choose only superior programs with educational values through a prudent choice of channels, even from those on AFKN (*The Kyunghyang Shinmun* 1974).

At the same time, many Japanese cartoons were aired on Korean terrestrial television on the pretext of being "made in America", indicating that the special status of "the American" was exploited to bypass prohibitions on Japanese popular culture.

> Children's programs on Korean television are being overwhelmed by American cartoons of heroic tales with preposterous adventures as their subject matter. Examples belonging to this category include *Mazinger Z*, *The Rough and Ready Cowboy*, *Planet Mask* (the above on MBC); *The Three Musketeers*, and *Adventure on Gaboten Island* (the above on TBC)... If Korean children psychologically distance themselves from reality while identifying themselves with the protagonists in American cartoons, they will find it difficult to shape their identity as Korean children. (*The JoongAng Ilbo* 1975c)

Simply classified, the "the American" flowed into public and formal space, while "the Japanese" entry was limited to private and informal space. However, these two spaces intersected in the Cold War cultural space and accumulated as shared experiences and memories. Just

50

as the U.S. military's PX was a Disneyland-like presence for many Koreans, situated domestically, albeit on the other side of a fence (Kim 2008: 132), for the young people of the day who lived under the control and oppression of a dictatorship, the various products of Japanese popular culture that they experienced in the public and private space stimulated their cultural desires for various cultural products denied by subjugation.

In other words, the conflicting cultural relationships that Korean society experienced around the American and the Japanese fragmented and diffused as multilayered desires and gazes in spaces where the two Others intersected and contradicted one another, such as television broadcasting and the PX, pirated music and videos, and coffee shops where music was played. The cultural identity that was created amid Korean popular culture and everyday consciousness was a product of conflicting and complicated experiences and strategies that cannot be understood merely in terms of public space suppressed by state power.

In Part Two, I will consider how Korean modernity was formulated in the nexus between "self-liberation" and "self-oppression" amid the multilayered intersection of 1) negating Japan (decolonization); 2) the dynamics of the Cold War (Americanization); and 3) the formation of domestic popular culture (industrial modernization), with a focus on the developmental dictatorship period from the 1960s to 1980s when the media culture industry was conceived and grew.

02

The era of the ban on Japanese popular culture

The Korean media space required
a mechanism of denial to carry out
its prohibition of Japanese culture.

Chapter **3**

MULTILAYERED SPILLOVER AND PROHIBITION

Experiences relating to Japanese culture were not only a de-colonizing process that sought to erase lingering remnants of Japan in Korea, but were also significantly shaped by the formation of a contemporary border between Japan and Korea as neighboring countries. The trans-bordering of radio waves from Japan highlights the limitations of the ban on Japanese popular culture.

Busan as a liminal space

The historical relationship between Japan and Busan

After independence, Busan, the second largest city in the south of Korea, was the space that most afforded a real sense of a substantial border with Japan. Goods and people from Japan had been "trans-bordering" across the sea since the colonial period, making Busan, even post-independence, an urban space in which "a fear of cultural absorption by polities of larger scale, especially those that are nearby" (Appadurai 1990: 32) was immediately felt, and where the ban on Japanese popular culture was a contemporary media phenomenon. It would be plausible to suggest that the principal pattern of the "ban on Japanese popular culture" – the tension between prohibition and trans-bordering – was created in Busan.

From the start, Busan had a unique historical relationship with Japan. The number of Japanese who had moved there via the sea route linking Nagasaki, Goto, Tsushima and Busan when the port at Busan opened in 1896 accounted for 25,641 of the approximately 47,000 residents of Busan. Having already developed a modern appearance

54

alongside the growth of the Japanese community, Busan was the city that was most markedly influenced by Japanese culture throughout the colonial period, and after independence it was perceived to be the "city where vestiges of the Japanese Empire continue[d] to be preserved" (*The Chosun Ilbo* 1948).

The following newspaper article points to the "vestiges of *waesaek*", "street urchins", "war refugees", and "profiteers" as four significant problems in Busan at the time; but all four were understood to result from a close connection with Japan, with the callous treatment of compatriots returned from Japan being seen as the main cause of street urchins, and smuggling between Japan and Busan as the primary factor in profiteering. On "vestiges of *waesaek*", the article explained:

> In the age of the Japanese Empire, Busan Port was a logistics base for imperial aggression, but post-liberation Busan Port made a splendid appearance as a base for overseas expansion of the new Korea… However, while on the one hand today's Busan is a place of heroic dynamism, it is also a hotbed of gloom and uncleanliness not seen elsewhere… After one alights from a train, it is Japanese that assaults the ear. I wonder why people use Japanese so much. Of course, it might be because there are so many compatriots that have returned to Korea from Japan. But when I see young people using Japanese without a care in the streets or at eating places, I not only naturally doubt their ethnic consciences, but also cannot help being astounded at their brazenness. Do they have no shame? And something else: things akin to Ministry of the Army noticeboards which the Japanese Empire left behind stand abandoned around the city, and restaurants serve nothing but Japanese food. Two years have passed already since the Japanese withdrew, have they not? Busan government authorities, of course, but ordinary compatriots, too! [You are] the disgrace of Busan (*The Kyunghyang Shinmun* 1947b).

Busan had occupied an important position from the colonial period, with the first regional broadcasting station in Korea being launched in Busan in 1936. During the Korean War, especially, the Busan broadcasting station became the Republic of Korea Central Broadcasting

Station (Busan Munhwa Broadcasting Corporation 2009: 16), attracting broadcasters and the cultural commentariat from all over the country to Busan (Roh 1995: 183). While the entire country was suffering from the ravages of war, special events that could not be held elsewhere formed the urban space that was Busan (Foundation for Broadcast Culture 2007a: 33).

In other words, Busan continued to be a border-like, or liminal space. The border between Japan and Korea was only one of many that were sustained and transgressed in Busan. All manner of borders – between colonial Korea and post-independence Korea; between the damage and the emergency demands brought about by the war; and between the periphery (Busan) and the center (Seoul), et cetera – were constructed and intersected in the urban space comprising Busan. Nevertheless, "spillover" from Japan was a particularly contentious form of trans-bordering in this liminal space.

Signal spillover

Spillover has given rise to diverse conflicts between developed and developing nations and can be understood as a universal cultural phenomenon in the media diffusion process. Arguably, "[e]ach nation should be entitled to monitor transborder information [and] monitor and control foreign media" (Roach 1993: 35–36). However, although based in a specific national economy and culture, the target market of broadcast signals is certainly not limited by any borders (Hall 1992), and their nature changes greatly according to "what kind of relationship they have with other countries". In other words, since the advent of mass media broadcasting, spillover has given rise to different perceptions, feelings and experiences depending upon the global and local dynamics generated by the historical context, while also producing shared experiences.

This means that analysis of Japanese spillover in Busan can help in understanding both the particular and universal characteristics of the relationship between Japan and Korea. In fact, places such as Ireland, Canada, Pakistan and Taiwan have treated "cultural trans-bordering" from close neighbors such as Britain, the U.S., India and Japan as a serious concern for national identity, and have sought various protective strategies such as prohibition of distribution and consumption. Having experienced the "internal spillover" via U.S. military broadcasting, Korea's cultural relationship with America shared various characteristics with other countries that "hosted" U.S. troops, including Japan, the Philippines, Taiwan, Germany, Italy and so forth. In short, the Korean experience of the Japanese spillover in Busan arguably shared many perceptions and emotions with other countries around the world during the mass-media diffusion from the 1960s.

Japanese radio signals and Korean broadcasting culture

The trans-bordering of radio broadcasts and Busan's media space

Among the first radio waves to arrive in Busan in the 1950s without any systemic regulation were Japanese broadcasts from the Kyushu region, which was geographically close. In particular, commercial radio broadcasting by Radio Kyushu (RKB), established in 1951, and Kyushu Asahi Hōsō (KBC), which began in 1954, influenced Busan's media and urban space (Park 1993: 21). That influence was a source of concern and prompted calls for a response plan to protect Korea's "wholesome national culture" from Japanese radio waves, which might negatively influence the Korean people's spiritual life (Busan Munhwa Broadcasting Corporation 2009: 19).

However, among Korea's broadcasters, perceptions of Japanese radio signals were more complex, including both a "sense of crisis" vis-à-vis Japanese commercial radio and a "sense of anticipation" towards the potential of domestic commercial broadcasting. In fact, spillover from Japanese commercial radio broadcasts had been the direct motivation for the establishment in April 1959 of Busan Munhwa Broadcasting (hereafter, Busan MBC), Korea's first commercial broadcasting station. *A 50-year History of Busan Munwha Broadcasting* outlines three points of justification for the establishment of Busan MBC.

1. To curb radio waves from Japanese commercial broadcasting that infiltrated Korea, there was a necessity to establish wholesome commercial broadcasting that would be able to deal with them. This was both a national and timely concern that transcended its business aspects.

2. Due to the influence of Japanese commercial broadcasting, the understanding of ordinary listeners in the Busan region towards commercial broadcasting was of a higher level than in any other domestic area. Accordingly, when establishing commercial broadcasting, the potential for it to grow as a business enterprise in concert with the industrial expansion of the Busan area was high.

3. In circumstances where all cultural activity was oriented towards the center, it was a trigger for the invigoration of regional culture. (Busan Munhwa Broadcasting Corporation 2009: 20)

Similarly, Kim Sang-yong, the founder of Busan MBC, referred to "the epoch-making launch of our country's first commercial broadcaster that can challenge Japanese commercial broadcasting" as the reason for launching Busan MBC and the main objective of its founding principles (Busan Munhwa Broadcasting Corporation 2009: 27). At the same time, with residents of Busan accustomed to Japanese commercial radio broadcasts, the Japanese broadcasters set the standard for judging the "commercial success" of domestic broadcasting. The greater the perceived threat of spillover, the higher the hopes were for domestic commercial broadcasting.

Chung Hwan-ok, who persuaded Kim Sang-yong to set up Busan MBC and joined him in the business, was the first to point out its commercial potential. Chung was a broadcasting engineer who had been employed by the Korean Broadcasters' Association (Joseon Bangsong Hyeobhoe/Chōsen Hōsō Kyōkai) during the colonial period. He observed that the variety of programming and advertisements in commercial radio broadcasting was far more open and oriented towards a popular audience than Japan's NHK (the national broadcaster) (Park 1993: 21; Busan Munhwa Broadcasting Corporation 2009: 19).

Choi Chang-bong, arguably the pioneer of Korean television broadcasting, head of broadcasting for Korea's first television station, HLKZ, Vice-president of KBS, and President of MBC, commented:

> On the occasion of the opening of Busan MBC, when I asked why it had been started, [I was told that the founder] launched it because, having heard advertisements being played at the end of every program on such stations as Kyushu Asahi and Radio Kyushu, [he] thought that it would make a [successful] business". (Foundation for Broadcast Culture 2007a: 118)

The launch of Busan MBC was a landmark in the history of advertising in Korean broadcasting. At the time, newspapers, magazines and other printed matter were the main media for publicity. The Korean broadcasters awoke to the concept of broadcast advertising through spillover from Japan (Broadcasting 1965). "Korean broadcasting set up its commercial broadcast system [in response to] the introduction of American and Japanese broadcasting systems, with a competitive setup comprising multiple private broadcasting stations with advertisements as their sole source of revenue" (Broadcasting Monthly 1971a).

Accordingly, radio signals from Japan, a source of social concern, were the most important site of learning for broadcasters in Korea. At the time, broadcasters in Busan reportedly listened to Japanese radio broadcasts on a daily basis. According to a 1958 chart for the government's public relations office, one of the allocated duties for the broadcasting management bureau was "listening to and studying broadcasts from foreign countries", but it was obviously Japanese broadcasts in Busan that comprised important sources (The Office of Public Information of South Korea 1958). According to Chung Sun-il, who was in charge of that task of "listening to and studying broadcasts from foreign countries", the program called "Jeongungnoraejarang" (Nationwide song contest), which was popular in Korea for decades, was launched in 1955 "after he heard a Japanese program called "Nodo jiman" in Busan that was broadcast every Sunday during the Korean War on Japan's NHK after a news program" (cited in Lim 2004: 382).

Among early broadcasters, such as Hwang Jung-tae, an important figure in launching the KBSTV station in 1962, many people improved their understanding of both the Japanese-language and foreign broadcasting in general through Japanese radio (Foundation for Broadcast Culture 2007c: 11).

The spillover from Japan influenced every domain of Korean broadcasting, from the format and sales of advertisements to the organization of broadcasting stations, as evidenced by reminiscences about the habitual practices of broadcasters of the day from Jeon Eung-deok, who held various positions, including head of the news division of Busan MBC and foreign correspondent for TBC based in Japan after working at Busan KBS. He says: "We were listening to Japanese radio to the extent that I remember most of the broadcast schedules, such as at 3 p.m. there was a song parade on Kyushu Mainichi Hōsō (RKB Hōsō), and on Kyushu Asahi Hōsō there was comic storytelling ... and [I remember] what was on NHK" (Foundation for Broadcast Culture 2007b: 77–78).

From 1961, when Korea entered the age of television broadcasting in earnest, that influence began to be a more serious problem. While viewers of Japanese television broadcasts comprised a unique media and urban space in Busan, those broadcasts exerted a huge influence on Korean broadcasting more generally, through being studied and imitated. In sum, for television broadcasting in Korea, which, as a measure of modernization, was a "political instrument" for the developmental dictatorship, spillover from Japan was simultaneously criticized as "cultural infiltration" and accepted as a model alongside the U.S. military's AFKN broadcasting.

The Japanese television boom in Busan

Korean television broadcasting began in earnest in the 1960s. After Park Chung-hee, had seized government in the May 16 military coup d'état, KBS was launched on 24 December 1961, followed by nine more commercial television stations launched in the 1960s. The Park regime actively utilized broadcasting to transmit public information, as well as continuing the publications and films that had been the primary means of publicity until the 1950s (The Ministry of Culture and Information of South Korea 1979: 46). Oh Jaekyung, who launched KBS as the martial regime's first civilian director (Department of Cultural Information), reminisced: "They [the regime], anticipated a powerful public information administration of me, but I did not think in that way. In public information, an indirect approach is more effective than a direct attack. When I researched how to convert a military revolution into a national revolution, I decided to establish a television station, which was the newest and most powerful form of media" (Oh 2003: 171–172). Clearly, the launch of KBS was intended as a propaganda machine for the dictatorship.

After three months of preparation, KBS began test telecasts on December 24, 1961, and formal telecasts on December 31. Those early Korean telecasts amounted to a "process of introducing broadcasting in the Third World, which had experienced a colonial period and was not equipped with its own ability to modernize" (Cho 2008: 257–258). From the very beginnings of its television broadcasting system, it relied on Japan and America in every element that comprised television broadcasting, including its system and management format, form of social usage, and so forth (Foundation for Broadcast Culture 2005: 1).

At the dawn of the Korean television age, spillover from Japan exerted a much greater influence than radio. Through the erection in September 1962 of a radio tower 130 meters tall, with an output of 300 watts in Izuhara, on Japan's Tsushima Island, NHK, NBC (Nagasaki Broadcast Company), RKB, and KBC signals from places such as Nagasaki and Fukuoka reached Busan and coastal areas in southern Korea. Their influence was felt immediately. As of 1962, in Busan where 500 or 600 television receivers had been installed in ordinary homes, a further 1,800 sets were added in the year immediately after the erection of the radio tower, and newspapers began to use the expression "boom" (*The Kyunghyang Shinmun* 1962a).

> The problem is the Japanese "boom" which is infiltrating the national lifestyle at a rapid pace. What about the influence exerted not only on adults, but on children, too, when they watch and listen to immensely interesting Japanese-style songs and films open to the public from early morning until late at night? If one thinks about the education of the second generation that loudly

advocates the purification of national culture, then it is sad even to imagine. Realistically, it seems that the side-effects of the Japanese television boom that is undermining the second generation has already become a social problem... Self-restraint by the residents could also be sought in order to block the Japanese "boom" permeating the southern region, but it would probably be necessary to work out terms for viewing state-run television broadcasts. (*The Kyunghyang Shinmun* 1963)

This situation was recognized even at the government level. People such as the Governor of Gyeongsangnam-do and its Chief of Police called for "self-restraint from ordinary television viewers for the sake of protecting the true national character, as well" (*The Kyunghyang Shinmun* 1962a); and the Director of the Department of Cultural Information reportedly issued a direct instruction to the head of Busan KBS, saying:

Now, Busan appears not to be our territory. The reality in which Japanese broadcasts are pervasive and people are straining their ears towards Japanese broadcasts in every household cannot be said to constitute our territory. I want you to go to Busan and bring Busan back into our territory! (Roh 1995: 374)

Image 3.1:
A Japanese television program shown on a television screen in Busan (*The Dong-A Ilbo* 1963b)

In those circumstances, the 1964 Tokyo Olympics were a media event that further spread the influence of spillover in Busan. Television sets sold out in cities all along the southern coast, from Busan to Masan, Chungmu, Jinhae, and Ulsan, and many visitors from Seoul and other areas stayed in hotels in the Busan area so they could watch the Tokyo Olympics (*The Kyunghyang Shinmun* 1964a). Throughout the Olympics, the city of Busan was crowded with people gathered in coffee shops and hotels that had televisions to view Olympic telecasts (*The Dong-A Ilbo* 1964b). One newspaper reported:

> President Park, visiting Busan on 23rd to attend the United Nations Ceremony in Memory of the Fallen, sat in front of a television set that evening in Room 510 of the Dongnae Tourist Hotel where he was staying, and watched a trans-bordering Japanese broadcast coming in across the Genkai Sea. (*The Kyunghyang Shinmun* 1964c)

This "Japan television boom" prompted an accelerated launch of television broadcasting in Busan, similar to the launch of Busan MBD in the age of radio. The beginning of broadcasts by DTV (later TBC TV) on 7 December 1964 as a privately-run television station was a typical example. The start of DTV broadcasts was extraordinary when one considers that it was not until 1968 that the state-run KBSTV set up a relay station in Busan. The speed with which it obtained permission to broadcast – only about a month – although beset with various issues (Foundation for Broadcast Culture 2007c: 11), was due to its stated aim of blocking Japanese signals, as can be inferred from the fact that it was given permission to broadcast on "Channel 7," which until then could pick up Japan's NHK. Likewise, for all domestic television in Busan, spillover from Japanese broadcasting was an important condition for the launch of television stations from the beginning.

According to *a 50-year history of Busan Munhwa Broadcasting*, even as late as the 1970 launch of MBC Busan television, whether it was public or commercial broadcasting, the justification was to prevent spillover from Japanese broadcasts being received in Busan. According to to the then director of technology of Munhwa Broadcasting, the aim of blocking spillover from Japan exerted a huge influence upon the broadcasting system.[1]

> At the time of its launch, Busan Munhwa Broadcasting's television channel was Channel 12. As had been the case with radio, at that time trans-bordering by Japanese television broadcasts in Busan and Gyeongsangnam-do [South Gyeongsang Province] was occurring in an unprotected manner, and Japanese broadcasts streamed from channels 7, 9, 11 and 13. Avoiding those Japanese channels, we made ours Channel 12. At the time, because Japan transmitted vertical signals, we also received permission for vertical signal transmission. As we were about to gradually build up output, we were told to change the frequency on November 30, 1971. This was tantamount to ordering us to change over to horizontal signal transmission to prevent spillover, due to Japan's being vertical. This is because signals coming vertically weaken when we respond with horizontal ones. The sole private telecaster in those days was Dongyang Broadcasting, and it was not powerful enough to prevent monopolization of the airwaves by Japanese commercial broadcasters. At the time, a television was a precious asset owned only by the wealthy, and town children would all come running to watch television, and sing Japanese songs. Young people copied Japanese fashions, and Japanese fashions, travelling via Busan, had occasion to be popular in Seoul. Accordingly, as in the case of the launch of a radio station in the past, the opening of the Busan Munhwa Broadcasting station carried the important meaning of stopping cultural encroachment from Japanese broadcasting. (Busan Munhwa Broadcasting Corporation 2009: 60)

---

1 Consequently, the station opened by changing the frequency from 7 to 9 due to strong opposition from people who had receivers capable of viewing Japanese television. It was not only the channel that was changed: as it was not possible to incorporate broadcasting equipment from a foreign country and production was therefore done by domestic assembly, output and so forth fell markedly short of what was originally planned, and in the end, broadcasting began with video output at 500 watts and audio at 250 watts. Its call sign, also, was HLKE (The 70-year history of Korean Broadcasting System Committee 1997: 395).

At the same time, though, spillover was a conduit for the absorption of Japanese technology. The telecast of the 1968 Mexico Olympics was one example. NHK signals from Tsushima were received by the microwave system of the "Busan relay station" (established April 1968) in cooperation with NHK, and then relayed to Seoul for broadcast to the entire country. In other words, even after plunging into the age of television, the influence of Japanese broadcasting continued, reaching right to the center, to Seoul's television broadcasting production system. All of the television stations in Seoul actively began to imitate and plagiarize Japanese broadcasting.[2]

Throughout its formative period in the 1960s, Korean television broadcasting, with a three-company system of KBS, MBC and TBC in place, aggressively copied, plagiarized, and incorporated Japanese television programs amid fierce competition for viewers. The imitation and broadcast of serial dramas and variety programs from Japanese television such as *Horoniga shō nandemo yarimashō* (Bittersweet Show, Let's try/show anything) and *Utatte odotte daigassen* (Big Singing and Dancing Contest) which had provided the impetus for Oya Soichi's critical comment about "The dumbing-down of the 100 million" (*Ichioku sō hakuchika*), was a common characteristic of the early period of Korean television broadcasting (Choi 1985: 369). The Korean broadcasting industry regarded the spillover from Japan as a tool that should be actively utilized, rather than interpreting it as mere "cultural invasion."

Immediately after the launch of MBC TV in 1969, an MBC compilation and production team monitored a week's worth of programs from Japan's public and commercial broadcasters with reception in Busan, and filled its schedule with imitations. In the advertising industry, also, one of the principal production methods was to dispatch key personnel from Seoul to Busan to monitor television broadcasts from Kyushu, and then bring their content to Seoul (Park 1993: 69). From the beginning, that "convention" was criticized because "the format of

---

2 "The audio was sent in the form of a relay transmission through an international telephone line by a Korean relay broadcast team dispatched to the site. In other words, it was in the form of a Japanese–Korean collaboration, so to speak, with the video being Japanese, while the audio was Korean" (The 70-year history of Korean Broadcasting System Committee 1997: 438).

television programs is mostly from Japan, and their entire composition and progression aspire to be like the Japanese ones" (*The Chosun Ilbo* 1974). Imitation and plagiarism became vital elements in forming the character of Korean television broadcasting, to such an extent that they are called the industry's "original sin" (Kim 2003: 207). In other words, even as Korea's broadcasting system was "Americanized" by directly absorbing the products of AFKN, its "Japanization" progressed through the translation and imitation of dramas and variety programs via spillover in Busan.

Everyday life in connection with Japanese television

At a research presentation of Korean newspaper studies held on 21 April 1973, results of research conducted in October 1971 on "the influence that Japanese television exerted upon the residents of the Busan region" were released. According to this survey, as many as 22% of people watched Japanese television in prime time, from 7 to 9 p.m., and half of them did not have any Japanese language ability. The report said: "As news and major variety programs are mainly aired in prime time, not only are there many viewers, and this directly impacts upon the government's publicity activities, but the advertisements greatly stimulate citizens' desires to purchase smuggled goods" (*The Dong-A Ilbo* 1973). That is to say, Japanese television had become the primary means of enjoying capitalist culture in everyday life.

Japanese popular culture was, therefore, one kind of "everyday culture", at least in Busan's urban space. Busan was the conduit for all manner of goods from Japan, with goods smuggled in from Shimonoseki, Kyushu, being actively consumed at the Kkangtong (Bupyeong) Market. This activity became even more lively around the time of the 1965 normalization of diplomatic relations between Japan and the Republic of Korea.

Recently, a month since the Korea–Japan Agreement came into force, in the international port city of Busan, Japanese monthly magazines, newspapers and the like have filtered in and are being sold in shopping districts in the city; and some city restaurants, eateries, coffee shops and so on are changing their décor or structure to so-called "*waesaek*"... In addition, "*waesaek*" has effectively already arrived in Busan, with Japanese people in Busan forming social groups for their own solidarity, et cetera, and spreading throughout the whole city. (*The JoongAng Ilbo* 1966a)

When TBC-TV conducted an opinion poll of Busan residents in 1967, the percentage who reported watching Japanese broadcasts had already reached 19.6% (*The JoongAng Ilbo* 1967c). A Mr. Bae Sun-hwan, who had been importing and selling Japanese books, magazines and so forth for several decades at the World Bookshop in Busan's second-hand book quarter, recounts his experience of spillover in the 1960s as follows:

> I did know that there were restrictions on Japanese popular culture such as comics and broadcasting. That was probably because President Park Chung-hee was worried that national spirit would grow lax. But in order to eat, we secretly brought them in, and watched television, too, because it was entertaining ... attaching the antenna under the eaves ... that's the way we did it in those days... I often watched [programs from] NHK, Fukuoka Broadcasting, and Osaka Broadcasting ... because Japanese radio wave technology was far more advanced at that time. And Busan was close, ... so families with money all had a Japanese television. (Busan Munhwa Broadcasting Corporation 2009: 20)

In other words, for the people of Busan in those days, Japanese broadcasting exceeded the level of simple contact with the signals that arrived, being also a means of leisure that they actively enjoyed. Just as the 1964 Tokyo Olympics was the key player in the Japanese television boom, Olympic relay telecasts were important media experiences in Busan. At that time, filmed scenes from the Tokyo Olympics were being broadcast on Korean television one day late due to a contract between KBS and NHK (Broadcasting 1964). However, in Busan, which was within reach of Japanese radio waves, it was possible to watch the transmissions in real time, as Bae Sun-hwan had done.

Especially because Japanese broadcasters showed a lot of sports telecasts, ... especially during the Asian Games and the Olympics in the 1960s, I installed an antenna to watch the activities of Korean athletes ... [and] everyone shed tears as they watched them... People would gather in Kkangtong Market and watch the Tokyo Olympics. I installed a Fuji brand antenna to see a clear image... It was amazing. (Bae, Sun-hwan. Interview. Conducted by Kim, Sungmin, 8 Aug. 2008)

In the 1970s, as television culture spread in earnest with the rapid increase in television receivers, Japanese broadcasting was accepted as everyday popular culture. Similarly, prior to the launch of color television in Korea in 1981, the consumption of color televisions swiftly expanded in order to watch AFKN and Japanese television. According to a survey by the Busan Municipal Office of Culture and Information, there were 40,000 color television receivers in the city by 1975. Demand

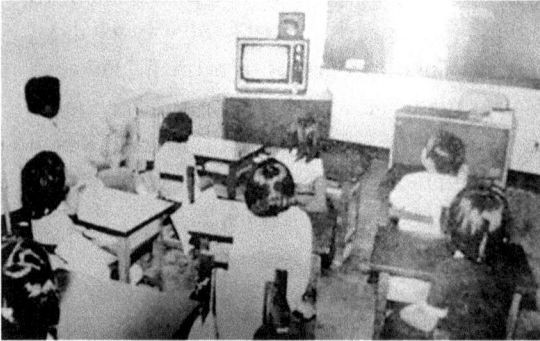

Image 3.2:
A classroom at Busan Japanese School where an audiovisual class is in progress (Busan Japanese School 1984)

Image 3.3:
'A family gathers to watch a Japanese TV manga movie program with clear images. Japanese characters are clearly visible and voices are audible.' (*The Dong-A Ilb* 1974)

was so strong that the sales price soared from 38.5 million won per unit to 120.15 million won per unit in one year.

For Japanese residents in Busan, too, watching Japanese television broadcasts was simultaneously a unique experience and part of everyday life. According to the School Handbook of the Busan Japanese School, which opened in 1975, Japanese television broadcasts had been used in classrooms since the school's establishment, thanks to spillover. Apparently, the sole overseas Japanese school where Japanese television broadcasts could be viewed was the one in Busan.

> The city of Busan has a population of approximately three million, and is the second-largest city in the Republic of Korea after Seoul. It is a nearby foreign city where Japanese television can be watched, it being about 50 kilometers from Japan's Tsushima. Its closeness to Japan also means that we can watch [Japanese] television, something that cannot be done at other Japanese schools, and so we use it extensively. (Busan Japanese School 1981)

In this manner, Japanese television signals crossing the border to Busan exerted enormous influence on the Korean television industry, while at the same time forming a media and urban space that differed from other areas. The continuing presence of many Japanese residents, the experience of the Korean War, the black market in smuggled goods, and various influences vis-à-vis the domestic radio and television industry all contributed to Busan's unique historical and geographical conditions and were extremely significant in the context of the ban on Japanese popular culture. A huge array of popular culture products from Japan, starting with spillover, and including magazines, books, popular music, videos, karaoke, and the like flowed in, contributing to the everyday media culture in Busan.

The multilayering of borders and the technology of bordering

The technology and legal system relating to spillover

As discussed, Busan provided a liminal space in the formation of Korean television broadcasting. The daily consumption of Japanese popular culture contradicted and conflicted with efforts to prohibit it. There are two aspects of this ambivalent modality that need to be understood.

First was the legal system, including the Broadcasting Act, the Radio Waves Act and similar prohibitions which contained no specific method for preventing spillover. In an effort to fill these gaps in the legal system, the city of Busan and the Korean government were limited to empty gestures such as the "No viewing Japanese telecasts movement." Second, while the spillover was understood on the one hand as "cultural invasion" which threatened national identity, on the other hand, it was a driving force for the development of Korean television culture.

Image 3.4:
Antennas installed in
a residential area for
viewing Japanese telecasts
(*The Kyunghang Shinmun* 1964b)

The most crucial element behind both aspects was technology. On the first, the technique of blocking signals called "jamming" and the insufficiencies of the legal system were compromised by active acceptance in everyday life, while on the second, the strong desire for advanced broadcasting technology collided with concerns about broadcasting as an ideological device. Technology for which the legal system had no response intersected with technology as means to modernization. One technological problem between Busan's and Japan's television broadcasting signals was the broadcasting transmission format. In the beginning, TBC employed a vertical polarization format, simply because Japanese signals were trans-bordering in the same format. When the three broadcasting stations adjusted their broadcast output in 1972, they consolidated their format to horizontal polarization. Moreover, each station tuned its frequency to a channel used by Japanese television. The object was to draw viewers from Japanese broadcasts to Korean broadcasts (Song 1995: 137).

Nevertheless, the audience for Japanese broadcasts just kept growing (*The Chosun Ilbo* 1975). The attempt to block Japanese signals by introducing a horizontal polarization format could be bypassed by simply installing a vertical antenna costing about 5,000 won (*The Dong-A Ilbo* 1974).

> Recently, the number of people watching AFKN-TV has rapidly increased. The fact that not only people who can comprehend English but even those who cannot are changing the channel to AFKN means that the number of people who have become tired of our television has grown rapidly. Not only that: so many people are watching Japanese television in coastal regions such as Busan, Jinhae, Ulsan and Masan that it would be no exaggeration to suggest that a "Japanese television culture zone" has been formed... The government is jamming Japanese television signals, but as our country does not have UHF (Ultra High Frequency) broadcasting, it is impossible to block Japanese UHF broadcasts, and because we do not broadcast in the daytime, we are defenseless against Japanese daytime television. (*The Kyunghyang Shinmun* 1979)

In other words, the technical and legal-system contradictions over Japanese spillover constituted one of the most significant conditions enabling the diffusion of Japanese television culture. Given such technical and legal-system contradictions, the government's desire to exploit television broadcasting for political propaganda, the commercial media's interests to profit from television, and the desire of the "masses" to consume television culture were intricately entangled.

Two kinds of spillover and the mechanism of bordering

In one sense, Busan's experience of spillover was common to many other countries. In the development of the broadcasting system, spillover significantly shaped the domestic broadcasting system and industry, in combination with: 1) the gaps in the legal system; 2) trans-bordering of the media space; and 3) individual consumption and the nationalist discourse that condemned it.

In another sense, though, spillover in Busan was unusual in that the trans-bordering occurred across two "borders": one between Japan and Busan, and another between Busan and Seoul. If we consider the former to have created a liminal media and urban space based on Busan's geographical and cultural distinctiveness (primary trans-bordering), then the latter – Seoul broadcasting stations imitating, translating and plagiarizing Japanese broadcasts – constituted "trans-bordering" in a different sense, stemming from the censorship process (secondary trans-bordering). These are markedly different phenomena. While Japanese programs being viewed in Busan were original and recognizable to anyone as being Japanese, the programs being viewed in homes elsewhere in the country via terrestrial broadcasts from Seoul were perceived as being Korean through various distortions intended to conceal their Japanese origins. That is, the trans-bordering in Seoul was a result of the government's efforts to impose a bordering mechanism.

Important factors to consider about this mechanism of bordering are language and generation. The "generation" of Koreans who had acquired Japanese language through their experience of colonialism (the Japanese-language generation) constituted the primary audience for Japanese radio and television in Busan in the 1950s and 60s, and thus introduced that system to Korean broadcasting. That is, amid the tension between trans-bordering and border-formation, generational differences between those who had Japanese language ability tied to their colonial experience and those who did not was an important factor.

A short story published in 1971 by Choi In-hoon (1936–2018), a novelist of the first generation born in post-independence Korea, well describes the complex mentality of young people vis-à-vis the older generation that enjoyed Japanese television broadcasts in Busan. The protagonist, a Korean university student born immediately after independence who, while witnessing Korean feelings of inferiority and desire, as well as subordinate consciousness towards America and Japan, agonizes about his own national identity and vents his complex feelings to a Japanese entrepreneur.

My father's face bears the marks of having been beaten by a Japanese teacher in the colonial period. The reason was simple. The Japanese teacher had set the memorization of your country's emperors as homework... My father had not memorized them... He chose names from the Joseon Dynasty. Due to that risky and foolish recklessness, he got two presents: expulsion from school and a scar on his face that even now he cannot erase. One more thing is about us ourselves. When we go early in the morning to an out-of-the-way coffee shop, usually your country's music is playing, our people in their forties lean their heads against the seat and lose themselves in that Japanese music. And that is not all. The residue of the seeds you sowed remain scattered, and touch the memories of old people... Once, I went to Busan and saw a samurai film from your country on television. At that time, the people who were watching television were ones who had spent their boyhood during your country's colonial period, and every time a samurai wearing geta clogs waved his sword, the atmosphere in the room seemed gradually to have returned to those sentimental and degenerate 1940s. (Choi 2002: 219)

Here, what the protagonist is recounting are his father's memories of having opposed education in Japanese and having tried to preserve Korean language and history in the colonial period, and his post-independence experience of people enjoying Japanese popular culture, in short, the ambivalence in the Korean society of his parents' generation. Clearly, given the prohibitions on Korean language and the Japanese education imposed during the colonial period, the disparity in perceptions and sentiments about Japanese popular culture between the generation that consumed it as culture itself and the generation that consumed it as foreign culture, or as Korean culture (in translation), was sharp.

In short, in contrast to other areas, the Busan experience indicates the importance of being able to understand Japanese in terms of the reception and prohibition of Japanese popular culture. As Japanese broadcasting crossed the border from Busan to Seoul by being translated, copied and plagiarized, the feelings of the so-called colonial generation who retained a sort of internalized affinity towards Japanese culture were excised. In other words, collective consciousness of those inculcated in Japanese culture from colonial days is clearly demarcated from the collective consciousness of the culture of a neighboring country, centering on familiarity with Japanese language.

Considering that until the 1980s, when there was no understanding or consideration of the concept of popular culture, the generation that experienced colonialism comprised the mainstream of a system which continued to generate a discourse based on a complex mixture of hatred and desire towards Japanese popular culture, represented by the idea of Japanese style as discussed in Chapter One, then the difference between the border between Busan and Seoul and the intergenerational border relating to Japanese language has generated a kind of "disparation" over Japanese popular culture amid the continuing formation of Korea's media and popular culture. Those who produced the discourses of prohibition and those who consumed Japanese-style culture despite the ban on Japanese popular culture were of the same generation, sharing perceptions and sentiments about Japanese style.

In this context, the contradictions inherent in the ban on Japanese popular culture through the 1960s and '70s generated a new attitude among the non-Japanese-language generation, creating fresh conflicts and contradictions. In other words, the ban on Japanese popular culture was not only a disparation between policy and industry, but also between discourse and practice, and between understanding and emotion within such diverse borders.

THE REPRODUCTION OF DESIRE AND PROHIBITION

A distorted effort to negate the inflow of Japanese popular culture enabled the ban on Japanese popular culture to operate in the South Korean mass media in the 1960s to 1980s. The result of this "mechanism of negation" was the continuous construction of an urban media space even while the ban on Japanese popular culture was being firmly maintained by South Korea's developmental dictatorship, when a great deal of Japanese cultural content flowed in by various means, including adaptation, translation, and rearrangement.

The mechanism of the ban on Japanese popular culture

The mechanism of negation

Television broadcasting was the media space in South Korea during the military dictatorship (from the 1960s to 1980s) that most clearly represented the mechanism of the ban on Japanese popular culture established around the time of the normalization of diplomatic relations between Japan and Korea. Belying the official history, in which Japanese broadcasting content was purported to be banned, much of it flowed in in diverse forms. The manner of its circulation and consumption was a product of the multilayered elements of the ban on Japanese popular culture, such as media practices, the production of social discourse, and the absence of legal proscriptions. However, as stated in the Introduction, the meaning, nature and efficacy of that ban cannot be appreciated if the cultural traffic is simply attributed to breaches of the ban. For one thing, it would be impossible to construct an identity based on the complete prohibition of cultural trans-bordering with an Other. From that perspective, the identity politics driving South Korea's relationship with Japan was ambiguous from the start.

I call the process of banning Japanese popular culture, a process in which border-formation and trans-bordering coexist, a "mechanism of negation". Freud understands "negation" to be a process of actively creating reality in such a way as to satisfy unconscious desires even while repressing them (Freud 2005: 89). If that requires deciding to prohibit a certain thing, "negation" will create the desired reality and allow it to persist. The process of assessing whether another culture is good or bad, beneficial or harmful, and deciding whether to accept or reject it, is a process of establishing borders between the inside and outside, making a distinction as to whether "I want to take this into me, or keep it out of me" (Freud 2005: 90–91). In contrast to exclusion accomplished through the stringent application of legal proscriptions, prohibition by means of negation can allow a prohibition even while accepting an outside culture simply by distorting the state of trans-bordering that is occurring. In other words, in a case of exclusion, trans-bordering would be punished as an infringement, but in a case of negation, the infringement itself becomes distorted.

What is termed "distortion" here is the omission, modification or regrouping of material through the operation of censorship – in short, the application of disguise and rearrangement (Freud 1991: 171–172). Censorship means not only direct erasure by a censor: it also acts to mask things by fear of censorship (Freud 2006: 155). In the context of the ban on Japanese popular culture, if we assume that the various moves of the immediate post-independence "movement to eradicate *waesaek* (Japanese style)" constituted a mechanism of exclusion, then the continuous inflow of various kinds of Japanese popular culture by means such as disguising its national origins and its translation, imitation, rearrangement and so forth, despite the ban on Japanese popular culture, can be understood as a "mechanism of negation" in which "distortion" was affected through censorship.

Revisiting the notion of "*waesaek*" discussed in Chapter One can help us to clarify this mechanism of negation. The (mechanism of) exclusion of Japanese popular culture during the liberation period and through the 1950s transformed into a mechanism of negation primarily through the discursive space comprising Japanese style. The border-crossing of a variety of Japanese popular culture was able to continue through the removal, disguise, and rearrangement of the Japanese style that was the focus of censorship. In short, distortion of the imports effectively negated the trans-bordering of Japanese popular culture.

Accordingly, it should be possible to apprehend how the ban on Japanese popular culture was fulfilled through a diverse mechanism of negation around inflow rather than a mechanism of exclusion which legally blocked any inflow. Although Japanese popular culture was officially banned in the South Korean media space, its diffusion was in fact necessary to fulfill various political and economic objectives, i.e., it could not be excluded. The "mechanism of negation" which allowed Japanese content to be disguised as South Korean unquestionably enabled cultural flow even while carrying out its prohibition. Both the "secondary trans-bordering" from Busan to Seoul discussed in Chapter Three and the television broadcasting of Japanese anime to be examined in this chapter were decidedly the result of the operation of a mechanism of negation. *Astro Boy* was presented as being South Korean by means of a mechanism of negation.

The developmental dictatorship and media culture policy

In the 1960s, cultural policy began to be developed in earnest along with a public information policy under the Park Chung-hee adminis-tration. These policies expressed a political ideology that was closely related to the maintenance of the regime, while defining the character and content of the nation. This was an attempt to simultaneously give form to South Korean citizens' consciousness and emotions (Oh 1998: 122), and to compensate for the regime's limited political legitimacy by emphasizing national culture. The cultural policy, however, "inherited the laws and ordinances from the colonial period without modification, and, rather than promoting and encouraging culture and the arts, focused more upon their policing and control" (Kim and Park 1998: 301).

The media, in particular, were subject to state control and cultivation based on nationalism. "Nation and state", "national identity", "patriotism" and so forth were political and cultural ideals that the military regime touted and which the media always had to respect (Cho 2008: 218). Public information policy emphasized the strict censorship and regulation of vulgar and decadent popular culture which was contrary to the regime's idealized, wholesome national character, on the one hand, while at the same time "strengthening the public function of such mass media as newspapers, broadcasting, and cinema" through the "preservation of traditional culture," the "wholesome introduction of foreign popular culture," "support for creative activities," and suchlike (The Ministry of Culture and Information of South Korea 1979: 81–90).

President Park Chung-hee's "words of encouragement" at the inauguration of the Ministry of Culture and Information blatantly express the regime's attitude towards the media.

> One might describe as "ground-breaking for the development of national culture" how in the present day, when culture and the arts have entered an age of popularization and the smoothness [of its accomplishment] has an inseparable connection with "mass communications," the cultural administration has shaken off the inefficiency of the binary division that existed hitherto between public information and culture, and has reestablished a new value system in national culture, while at the same time assembling a unified structure that can demonstrate the powerful authority which actively supports it… I hope that commentators and cultural practitioners who engage in all kinds of "mass communications," also, will understand the direction of the government's new policy, and take the lead in building a wholesome social ethos based upon the awareness that everyone shares social responsibility. (The Ministry of Culture and Information of South Korea 1979: 446)

The Park regime had been especially interested in television as a medium since the 1961 coup d'état. With the objective of "autonomously maintaining the public nature of broadcasting and its order and dignity," the South Korean Broadcasting Ethics Committee was inaugurated in 1962 to regulate television broadcasting in accordance with the Broadcasting Act of 1963. In the seventeen years until 1979, the South Korean Broadcasting Ethics Committee conducted deliberations over a huge number of cases (22,964), including 6,903 cases of regulation vis-à-vis broadcasting stations; 238 cases of penalties against connected persons; 1,759 cases of warning, rectification, or recommendation; 1,172 cases of decision to ban broadcast of songs; 1,493 cases of decision to ban broadcast of advertisements; 41 cases of review; 156 cases of complaint; 10,930 cases of deliberation on broadcasting of television advertisements; 272 cases of deliberation on foreign film scripts and foreign video recordings for television; and so forth (The Ministry of Culture and Information of South Korea 1979: 208–209).

It was nigh impossible for television broadcasting to express any views that clashed with state guidelines, because the South Korean television broadcasting network in the 1970s was a product of the political considerations of state power. In 1971, as the aims of broadcasting, Culture and Information Minister Yun Joo-young called for: 1) expanded transmission of national culture; 2) preventing the injudicious importation of foreign culture; 3) suppression of foreign language lyrics in popular songs; and 4) exclusion of vulgar or low-quality programs (*Broadcasting Monthly* 1971b).

However, solely in the case of entertainment programs, there were many occasions when the demands of the state and the interests of broadcasting were necessarily at odds. Television stations, which had absolutely no autonomy on a political perspective, being unable to reject the various demands of the government, endeavored to respond positively as far as this did not contradict market strategy. However, when this restrained market strategy, they showed a tendency to respond in an extremely negative manner (Cho 1994: 239). Especially after the 1973 corporatization of KBS, which had been the state-run broadcaster, heated competition for audience ratings between the three broadcasters exerted a huge influence upon broadcast programming and production. This competition became the driving force behind increasing commercialism in television broadcasting. Thus, from the 1970s, when Korea's industrial modernization unfolded in earnest, the government's "authoritarian cultural policy" – that is, regulation by means of government-regulated cultural and bureaucratic authoritarianism – found itself in a mutually tense relationship with the media's "commercialism" with its needs for commercialized popular culture (Lee 1984: 257).

Under Chun Doo-hwan's military regime (1980–86), the state also sought to mobilize the mass media to its own ends. Through its 1980 measures to structurally reorganize the news media, the Chun regime enforced strict censorship and regulation of the news media by means such as abolishing and amalgamating fourteen newspaper companies, one news agency and two broadcasting stations, while at the same time adopting a so-called "3S [Sex, Screen, Sports] policy" of less stringent censorship relating to sex in films, launching a series of professional sports, and other measures seeking to depoliticize culture (Kang 2003: 54). Thus, during the Chun regime, media culture was riddled with political sentiment, as shown by Chun Doo-hwan's directive:

> The Ministry of Culture and Information, not the KCIA (Korean Central Intelligence Agency), is to be responsible for and promote issue of the domestic press, and the Ministry of Culture and Information possesses high-level political sense. It is to secure outstanding, capable personnel with deep knowledge in each field. (Kim 1989: 161–162)

In Article Eight of the Constitution of the Fifth Republic, the Chun administration strove to legally implement state control vis-à-vis culture by stipulating that "[t]he state should make efforts towards the inheritance and development of traditional culture and the promotion of national culture," and "political efforts for cultural expansion."

The reason the military regimes both restricted the concept of "national culture" in cultural policy to "traditional culture" was that they had scant political legitimacy, having reduced the meaning of "national" to a powerful anti-communist ideology defined by the north–south situation. Violent suppression in the 1980 Gwangju Uprising, in which "national" and "national culture" were the most important issues for those opposing the government, was a crucial factor in the Chun regime's cultural policy (Koo 1998: 6). In other words, in the developmental dictatorship period – when the nation was defined by the north-south division, and the processes of decolonization and modernization were increasingly intertwined – the words "nation" and "national" had themselves become a site of conflict and contradiction.

In this way, the dictatorships' media and cultural policies were shaped by three concerns: 1) cultural policy that emphasized national culture; 2) strict regulation of the media; and 3) tacit approval of commercialism.

The issue of banning Japanese popular culture permeated these three areas in an ambiguous manner. One might expect a cultural policy that emphasized national culture to target Japanese popular culture for strict control, but the toleration of commercialized media created demand for the inflow of Japanese popular culture.

From the initial establishment of television stations, television broadcasting was seen as a strategic means for preserving, maintaining and expanding national spirit and traditional culture. Under an authoritarian regime that had defined nationalism in terms of the north/south issue – anti-communism and anti-North Korean sentiments – television broadcasting had to make the state-defined nationalism its most sacred pillar. But at the same time, strong commercial forces appeared amid a system of fierce competition. At a glance, these forces of nationalism and populism seem to have been in conflict, but in fact, they shared the same locus of "cultural popularization" (Cho 2008: 219–220).

The ban on Japanese popular culture as a legal system

So, what was the legal status of the ban on Japanese popular culture in the 1960s to the 1980s, when the South Korean media industry took shape?

The ban on Japanese popular culture was not established through concrete laws and ordinances explicitly mentioning Japan, such as a "Japanese Popular Culture Prohibition Act." It was not unified in a single piece of legislation, but rather was in fragments scattered through laws and ordinances relating to popular culture in general. Let us examine those in order.

First, Item 2 of Article 19 of the "Public Performance Act" of 1961 stipulates "restriction of public exhibition of foreign performances", specifying that it is "not possible to publicly exhibit foreign performances that risk harming the national spirit, [and/or] violate public order and good morals." Article 7 of the "Act Relating to Importation and Distribution of Foreign Publications" (1973) contains an item called "Foreign publications recognized as liable to injure public safety and public morals." In both of these cases, although Japan is not explicitly named, their formulation was such that they provided grounds for banning Japanese popular culture. Moreover, Article 5 of the "Broadcasting Act" (1963), called "Ethical stipulation," stresses the importance of "Cultivation of national initiative," "Creative development of national culture," "Guidance of children and youth," "Purity of family life," and so forth. In addition to those, although less directly because they did not specify "foreign," Article 13 of the "Film Act" (1966), Article 10 of the "Act Pertaining to Phonogram Recording" (1967), and other legislation stipulated that "corruption of the national constitution," "national sentiment," "social order," and "national spirit" were grounds for prohibition.

How, then, did laws and ordinances which did not specify Japan actually impose a ban on Japanese popular culture?

The following record demonstrates that the legal system at that time lacked substantial efficacy vis-à-vis the ban on Japanese popular culture. In 1968, the governor of Gyeongsangnam-do enquired about the legality of "public exhibition at cultural centers [munhwawŏn] of cultural films provided by the Japanese Consulate that have not been censored by the Ministry of Public Information." A legal officer from the Ministry of Public Information replied:

> In accordance with Items 2 and 3 in Article 11 of the Motion Picture Law, all films must undergo censorship by the Minister of Public Information prior to their exhibition, and as a mandatory stipulation, there must be no exception to that same stipulation. Accordingly, as the exhibition of [the films] in question is considered not to be possible, I shall directly issue notification of that specific matter. (The Bureau of Judicial Affairs of South Korea 1968)

Basically, the reason given for refusing permission to show Japanese films was not that they were Japanese, but that they were uncensored. From this example, it can be read that there were clear limits to directly regulating Japanese popular culture through the application of popular culture laws and ordinances that did not specify Japanese popular culture. Moreover, in 1971, the Ministry of Internal Affairs enquired whether outdoor advertisements explicitly promoting a "technical partnership with Aji-no-moto" could be restricted "as something that injures national identity?" The Ministry of Culture and Information replied that "in the laws and ordinances under this Ministry's jurisdiction, there is no legal basis enabling the implementation of regulation to that [matter]" (The Ministry of Home Affairs of South Korea 1971).

Accordingly, the ban on Japanese popular culture could be described as a social norm with an extremely vague legal basis. In 1966, the year after the normalization of diplomatic relations between Japan and Korea, President Park stated: "Since the normalization of diplomatic relations between the Republic of Korea and Japan,

Table 4.1: List of permitted importers of foreign periodicals

License number	Importer	Newspaper		Magazine		Place of Export
		Number of titles	Number of copies	Number of titles	Number of copies	
1	Dongnam Publication Trade Co., Ltd.	11	4,160	405	47,275	Japan
2	Dongyang & Co., Ltd.			75	13,400	Japan
3	Uil Culture Company	2	130	82	60,720	West*
4	Foreign Publication Agency	7	560			West*
5	Charles Foreign Agency	1	500			US
6	Daeyang Publication Company			8	1,500	Europe
7	Sambon Trading Company			3	1,500	US
8	Wonchang Publication			26	5,100	Europe
9	Beoma Publication public corporation			13	3,100	China

* "West" = France, Germany, Italy, U.K., U.S., Hong Kong, etc.

members of our nation themselves must prevent the intrusion of Japanese culture such as records and magazines" (*The JoongAng Ilbo* 1966c). Thus, this normalization of diplomatic relations, which the President declared "an unprecedented shift for state development and national glory" (*The Chosun Ilbo* 1966), shunted the responsibility for upholding the ban on Japanese popular culture from the state to the civilian population.

In fact, what was prohibited seems not to have been stipulated, either. For example, while President Park pointed to the circulation and consumption of Japanese magazines as an important example of "the intrusion of Japanese culture," a Ministry of Culture and Information publication from June 1971, entitled *List of permitted importers of foreign periodicals* (see Table 4.1), reports the numbers of Japanese magazines imported in a month.

According to these records, the variety of newspapers and magazines being imported from Japan was huge, even in comparison with other countries. The contents, too, indicate that all kinds of publications were included, from newspapers: *Asahi Shinbun* (1,200 copies), and *Yomiuri Shinbun* (1,100 copies) to weekly magazines such as *Shūkan Yomiuri* (350 copies) and *Shūkan Bunshun* (250 copies) and specialist magazines in fields such as science, machinery, architecture, economics, medicine, education, law, printing, the arts, sports, leisure, hobbies, agriculture and fisheries, and radio. Literary, fashion, lifestyle and hobby magazines with the largest circulations were *Bungei Shunjū* (1,900 copies), *Sōen* (1,500 copies), *Shufu no Tomo* (1,300 copies), *Shufu to Seikatsu* (1,300 copies), *Fujin Kurabu* (Women's Club) (1,200 copies), *Wakai Josei* (Young Ladies) (1,300 copies), *Rīdāzu Daijesuto* (Reader's Digest) (1,300 copies), *Doresumēkingu* (Dressmaking) (1,200 copies), *Asahi Kamera* (Asahi Camera) (1,100 copies), *Bijutsu Techō* (Art Notebook) (800 copies). Other magazines, including *Eiga Jōhō* (Movie Pictorial) (150 copies), *Kindai Eiga* (Modern Movies) (50 copies), *Kinema Junpō* (Movie Times) (twice monthly quantity: 50 copies), and *Terebijon Eiji* (Television Age) (50 copies), which were supposedly prohibited because of content related to cinema and television, were also granted import permission. Of these, *Sukurīn*'s (Screen) 1,200 copies placed it in the upper ranks of magazines. In short, in an environment where, at least in principle, there was a prohibition on reading Japanese magazines, Japanese magazines were being legally imported in huge numbers, demonstrating that the ban on Japanese popular culture was not a rigorous legal mechanism.

In fact, various actions that might be described as breaches of the ban were not actually illegal, because there were no authorities, administrative bodies, or police to enforce laws concerned with the inflow and consumption of Japanese popular culture. Furthermore, as South Korea had not yet signed the two international copyright treaties – the Universal Copyright Convention (UCC) and the Berne Convention (for the Protection of Literary and Artistic Works) – it was not regulated by international law, either.

In such circumstances, the ban operated as a "discourse" that problematized the circulation and consumption of Japanese popular culture. Arguments within South Korea in favor of the ban on Japanese popular culture can be summarized broadly into four categories: 1) discourses on national identity; 2) discourses on anti-Japanese sentiment; 3) discourses on protection of children and youth; and 4) discourses on protection of domestic culture industries. That is to say, from the 1960s onwards, with the ubiquitous trans-bordering of Japanese popular culture, the ban on Japanese popular culture was reduced to discourses that problematized this situation. Yet, the formal and informal importations that occurred in those circumstances were not simple infringements of the ban, either. As mentioned at the beginning of this chapter, the consumption of Japanese anime and manga via South Korean television broadcasts and magazines was not a process of direct trans-bordering, for these products were rearranged and transformed to disguise their Japanese origins.

Japanese anime and South Korean television broadcasting

Trans-bordering television anime and the ban on Japanese popular culture

It goes without saying that the most important communications medium in South Korean society in the 1970s was television. The number of television receivers, only 120,000 in 1968, soared due to the government's active diffusion policy, reaching 1.2 million sets five years later, in 1973, and 5 million in 1978 (Foundation for Broadcast Culture 2005: 14). In concert with this, children began to turn their attention from comics to television (*The Chosun Ilbo* 1970).

The many televised anime programs, such as *Astro Boy* and *Tiger Mask* were typical of children's culture in that new age of television. They were all marked by the endeavor to erase their Japanese origins and style by changing the context, the name of the lead character, and so on.

The first thing to be carried out was a "change of nationality". As the following newspaper article from the time of initial airing of *Tiger Mask* shows, many works at the time were introduced as either U.S.-made or domestically-made anime.

> TBC [Tongyang Broadcasting] will air a new manhwa film [animation],[1] *Tiger Mask*, every Wednesday from 7 o'clock... Ten years ago, there was a boy named Tom at an orphanage in a village in the United States... The tales of the boy Tom's successes are sure to give children knowledge and courage. (*The JoongAng Ilbo* 1971a)

The 1971 "Fact-finding Investigation Report on South Korean manga" reported that "Among the manga surveyed, there were ones in which Japanese athletes sporting the South Korean national flag appeared" (*The JoongAng Ilbo* 1971b), which was a clear result of the process of changing the nationality of Japanese manga. *Mazinger Z* was also initially introduced as an "American-made science fiction manga film".

---

1 As the expression "anime" did not exist at the time, the terms "manhwa [comic] films," "manhwa," "films" and similar were employed. The translation uses these terms only in direct citations.

Note, however, that "anime" is Japanese for "animation", and thus the two words are often used synonymously, in contrast to the English norm of reserving anime for the subset of animations that are Japanese made, or made in the Japanese style. For most purposes in this chapter this distinction is unimportant, but occasionally, the term animation will be used to distinguish non-Japanese animation from Japanese anime.

> MBC TV will air the science fiction manga film, *Mazinger Z*, from
> 11th. This work, a production of the "American Pictures Company",
> is an educational film incorporating outer-space science that will
> give children interest and knowledge. (*The JoongAng Ilbo* 1975b)

The popularity of *Mazinger Z*, according to one newspaper, "ignited
an SF anime boom" in South Korea (*The Kyunghyang Shinmun* 1976),
which is also described in a 30-year history of Munhwa broadcasting:

> Among anime that began in 1975, the whirlwind hit *Mazinger Z*
> dominated popularity among children. The feature of *Mazinger
> Z*, created by a man called Soedori, was that a person would
> enter the head of a robot and control it, and Soedori's excellent
> manipulation and high-level technology vanquished Dr. Hell's
> cyborg, the symbol of evil, giving [the viewer] keen pleasure. (The
> 30-year History of Munhwa Broadcasting Corporation Committee
> 1992: 738)

A method employed along with a "change of nationality" was active
"translation." In *Mazinger Z*, the name of the lead character in the
original version, Kabuto Kōji, was changed to a Korean-language
name, Soedori. Such translations resulted in even works that were
explicitly introduced as U.S.-made being perceived as being made in
South Korea. Therefore, most Korean viewers could not recognize
the works as Japanese. Young people even sang the theme song of
Mazinger Z at soccer games in Japan and Korea. A 1975 analysis of
television programs of the time in *Broadcasting Ethics*, for example,

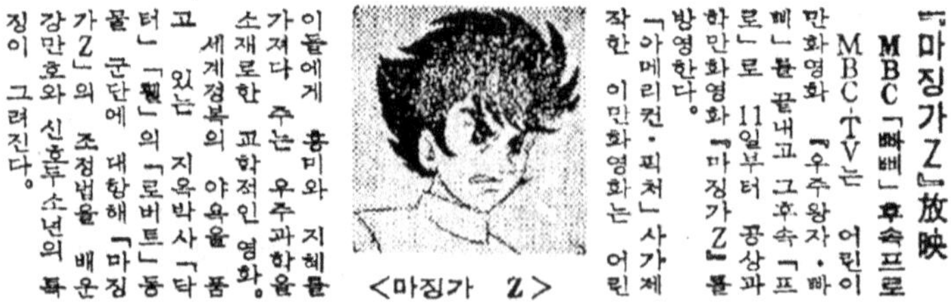

Image 4.1: An article introducing *Mazinger Z* as U.S.-made
(*The JoongAng Ilbo* 1975b)

classifies animated programs into "science fiction," "fairy tales," "exploration and/or adventure," "westerns" and so on, and points out such problems as "there are many that make war their subject matter," they "lack reality," there is "overuse of imported expressions" and "use of violent language" (Broadcasting Ethics 1975), but omission of any mention of their nationality was probably due to a public assumption that these were not Japanese works.

As for theme songs, it was common for the melody to be retained, while the lyrics alone were translated. Music critic Lee Young-mi describes her experience at the time as follows:

> When I was small, I had an intriguing experience relating to the theme song from *Golden Bat*. One day, I was lined up in front of the television with my older brother and younger sister in time for the broadcast of *Golden Bat*... Huh? The theme song that played after the cool intro had Japanese lyrics! It seems they probably played the wrong tape for the theme song. There must have been an uproar at the TV station because of this serious broadcasting error. Not being able to understand Japanese, we could not know how closely the Japanese lyrics matched the lyrics in our language, but we were able to hear the words "silver baton" clearly [the silver baton being the weapon that Golden Bat used], ... and we surmised that most of the Japanese lyrics had been directly translated. (Lee 2002: 135–136)

As the young Lee had guessed, the Korean version of *Golden Bat*'s theme song (aired from 1967) had been broadcast with translated lyrics set to the original melody. Among the many works that retained the original melody for the theme song were: *Astro Boy* (1970–), *Mazinger Z* (1975–), *Candy Candy* (1977–), *Eagle 5* (1979–), and *Galaxy Express 999* (1981–). What is intriguing in this process is the shift in the critical evaluation of these products. As mentioned, *Mazinger Z* was positively appraised as being "educational, with space science as its subject matter which provided children with interest and knowledge" when it was introduced as being U.S.-made (*The JoongAng Ilbo* 1975b), but at the same time, in a context where their made-in-Japan status was gradually being exposed by newspapers and gaffs such as the one Lee described, "anime that gave dreams and hope to children" began to be seen as "low-quality Japanese-style culture". For example, Korean newspaper *The JoongAng Ilbo* pointed out that *The Rough and Ready Cowboy, The Adventures of Hutch the Honeybee, Three Space Musketeers* and others were Japanese-made. Furthermore, the paper argued, an easy way to tell if anime imported via U.S. film companies were actually Japanese made was "if the movement of the characters was somewhat impaired, and they had a Korean name, then it would unmistakably be a Japanese product" (*The JoongAng Ilbo* 1975a).

As the Japanese origins of television anime became generally well-known in the 1970s, it became an issue for the government. The 1976–77 *Broadcasting Ethics Commission Evaluation Report* described anime such as *Sally the Witch* and *Marine Boy* as innocent or science fiction anime, and noted they came from overseas. However, the National Parliament's Culture and Public Information Committee was quite explicitly informed that "most manga films in children's program timeslots [we]re Japanese or foreign." Moves to regulate foreign culture were extended to programs for children, and eventually the Broadcasting Ethics Committee began to discuss a policy of replacing foreign-produced children's programs with domestically produced works (Republic of Korea National Parliament 1978). In Question Time in November 1976, the South Korean national parliament problematized the Japanese origins of television anime in the following manner.

> Song Hyo-soon (National Parliamentarian): In current television broadcasting, programs aimed at children are aired from 6 pm until 7 pm, but the anime that appear there are all Japanese ones, with the existing video, and only the audio dubbed in Korean… I want them to stop that immediately, even from tomorrow!
>
> Kim Sung-jin (Minister for Culture and Information): You said that Japanese cartoons are being aired in children's timeslots. I shall take action on this problem by undertaking a thorough crackdown through the Broadcasting Ethics Committee to prevent such a thing from occurring. (Republic of Korea National Parliament 1978)

However, despite the Minister's declaration to take action, Japanese anime continued to account for an overwhelming proportion of animated television programming from the mid-1970s. The television program schedule of the day shows that eight out of the eleven animated programs aired throughout 1976 were made in Japan (two were U.S.-made; one was European-made), and in 1977, ten out of fifteen works aired were made in Japan (four U.S.-made, one European-made). This is indicative of how willingly television broadcasters and audiences accepted Japanese popular culture, while simultaneously demonstrating that commercial forces and popular desire disregarded the semi-authoritarian influence of the state.

Choi Deok-su, who rose through the ranks of the KBS Television Production Department – head in 1961, Vice-president/General Manager in 1973 – explained the broadcasting of Japanese anime at that time.

> When purchasing Japanese anime, I was aware of its nationality. I also knew that the sales agencies sometimes used American names at their convenience, ... because the audience ratings would rise. There were no major restrictions within the broadcasting station as to airing Japanese anime. Competition was fierce, too, and the producer's position was that they wanted to air anything that would mean even one more person would watch it. (Foundation for Broadcast Culture 2007a: 417–418)

Thus, from the 1970s onwards, despite an implicit ban on Japanese popular culture with no direct legislated regulatory basis, television broadcasting willingly disguised the Japanese origins of programs in order to import and broadcast them.

This was primarily driven by the pursuit of audience ratings, but expense was also a significant factor. At that time, the price of imported anime was fairly cheap in comparison to films and television dramas, and at 350,000–700,000 won compared to the estimated 15 million won to produce anime domestically, the local production of television anime by domestic broadcasting stations was deemed to be "unthinkable" (*TV Guide* 1981; *The Dong-A Ilbo* 1982).

Analysis of the television animations aired annually in the 1980s, according to television programming schedules, reveals that Japanese-made anime accounted for an overwhelming proportion: 20 in 1981 (6 U.S.-made); 19 in 1982 (4 U.S.-made); 21 in 1983 (6 U.S.-made); and

14 in 1984 (8 U.S.-made). This phenomenon was problematized in the *Broadcasting Commission* journal.

> The [genre] that has many problems is children's anime. Examples of films that projected an opaque image in the aspects of nationality and emotion are *Galaxy Express 999* and *Queen Millennia*. In the case of *Galaxy Express 999*, it is supposedly in the category of a science fiction film adapted to the space age, but its half-baked philosophy of life and the relationship between the leading characters Cheori and Maetel was handled vaguely, while in the case of *Queen Millennia* it was more serious, because it was cancelled in mid-season as it was rumored to be a work based on Japanese mythology. (Broadcasting Commission 1983; annotation added.)

However, although Japanese anime was criticized by broadcasting experts, such critique hardly ever took the form of actual debate. Conversely, there was also a shortening of the time-lag between the start of telecast of new works. For example, whereas Mazinger Z aired in Japan from 1972 to 1974, it was not aired in Korea until 1975. In contrast, *Alps Story: My Annette*, which was aired in Japan from 9 January to 25 December, 1983, began broadcasting on MBC in South Korea on 4 November, 1983.

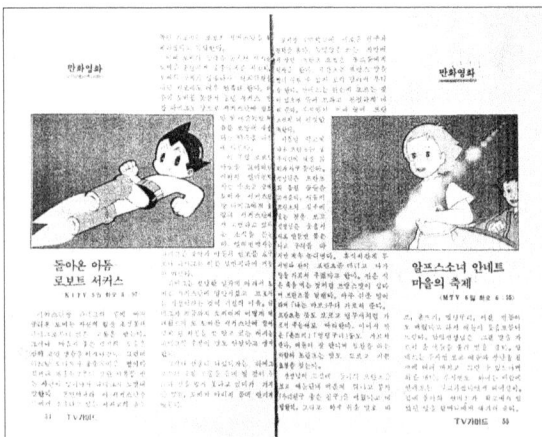

Image 4.2:
Left: *Astro Boy*; right: *Alps Story: My Annette*. (*TV Guide* 1983)

The structure of Japanese–South Korean television anime production

On 17 July 1968, the front of Seoul's Kukje Theater was bustling, with a 30-metre-long queue of children. The 1,700 or so tickets had already been sold out at 8:20 in the morning for the first screening of the previously mentioned television anime, *Golden Bat* (*The Kyunghyang Shinmun* 1968b).

The mega-hit anime, *Golden Bat*, was introduced as the first anime produced by TBC-TV (Tongyang Broadcasting), but being a joint production with Japan, it was effectively a Japanese product. Advertisements for the feature film version listed the production companies as TBC and Dai-ichi dōga, but the South Korean contribution to the production was simply "outsourcing." Following the normalization of diplomatic relations between Japan and Korea, the director, Morikawa Nobuhide, was sent to South Korea to make *Golden Bat* and *Humanoid Monster BEM* in a four-year joint operation with a South Korean labor force. Dai-ichi dōga, the Japanese production company, took responsibility for the planning, scenario, storyboard and so on, while the Video Production Department of South Korea's TBC created the cells (Seo 2009: 86–88).

This "outsourcing" of production enabled *Golden Bat* – which was Japanese-made in every respect, including story structure and direction – to be aired on South Korea's TBC. Choi Deok-su, who served as TBC's inaugural Head of the Programming Bureau, spoke as follows about *Golden Bat*.

> It was TBC-TV that made the first anime. That was *Golden Bat*. The drawings are called cells, and I took those cells to Osaka Television. The next [we made] was *Humanoid Monster BEM*. After the team who made those anime

Image 4.3:
A newspaper advertisement for the theatrical version of *Golden Bat* (*The Kyunghyang Shinmun* 1968a)

93

dissolved, [those works] became the foundation of South Korean anime. The anime from Tongyang Broadcasting (TBC) were from the so-called Video Department, and their role was huge. (Foundation for Broadcast Culture 2007d: 246)

As Choi Deok-su remarks, the Video Department of TBC was dismantled, and the Japanese–Korean co-production system that had produced *Golden Bat* was abandoned. *Golden Bat* and *Humanoid Monster BEM* were historically significant as "Japan–South Korea co-productions," but without diversifying the joint production mechanism, "outsourcing" became entrenched, and, combined with the previously discussed cost of production, the South Korean television anime industry became overly reliant on outsourcing, both for Japanese and local-content. The twenty years between the opening of *Golden Bat* and the first wholly South Korean-made television anime program, produced and aired in 1987, indicate the lasting influence that decision had on the industry.

However, from the perspective of South Korean popular culture, the effects of these four years of experience were various and cannot be assessed in terms of a simple dichotomy of "positive" and "negative." *Golden Bat*'s production, distribution and consumption symbolized the dissatisfaction and anxiety around the normalization of diplomatic relations between Japan and Korea in the late 1960s amid lingering cultural sensitivities in South Korea's relationship with Japan, the Other. If one understands outsourcing not as cultural subordination, but as the introduction and formation of popular culture, then *Golden Bat* was the first post-independence experience in which Japanese popular culture was officially introduced to South Korea.

However, as previously argued, the broadcast of Japanese television anime cannot be understood simply as a breach of the ban on Japanese popular culture. In effect, in the absence of legally enforceable measures, a mechanism of negation functioned to uphold the ban by importing, translating, and disguising the origins of Japanese anime. Whether it was a case of distribution via a third country or an outsourcing structure, Japanese anime always trans-bordered, disguised as something that was not made-in-Japan.

While television broadcasting was a potent means of promoting growth and spreading propaganda, artificially legitimizing the regime in power, as commercial media it not only provided national entertainment but was also a vehicle for de-politicization and de-ideologization. In television programming, a "paratactic binary structure" combining state and media (Cho 1994: 44–46) was produced by capital taking the initiative. Under that binary structure, the original version of *Astro Boy, Tetsuwan Atomu* negated violations of the ban on Japanese popular culture by trans-bordering in the guise of the Korean version of *Astro Boy, Ujusonyeon Atom.*

Censorship and the discourse on prohibition

Amid such trans-bordering, social discourse performed the function of censorship. The media, in particular, reproduced negative perceptions of Japanese popular culture, while provoking a widespread moral panic about contact with Japanese popular culture – in short, what Freud described as "criticism by society that is regressively reproduced" (Freud 2003: 25). Newspapers were the medium that most actively provoked that moral panic.

Newspapers had been the state's most important avenue for promoting nationalist propaganda in the post-independence period of state-formation in South Korea, and willingly played their part in producing an anti-Japanese discourse. Immediately following independence, newspapers promoted the elimination of Japanese style from Korean society, saying: "given that it is the result of having been oppressed for a long time, even one day sooner ... we must eliminate *waesaek*" (*The Chosun Ilbo* 1946). Around the time of the normalization of diplomatic relations between Japan and Korea, almost twenty years later, when trans-bordering by Japanese popular culture was both increasing in volume and becoming more brazen about its national origins, newspapers declared a new "Japan boom," which they portrayed as "the return of imperialism," as noted in the following article.

The "Japan boom" that had arisen at one period in the world of popular songs began to appear again from the publishing world. There is a flood of all kinds of Japanese publications – newspapers and books, of course, but even illegally imported sexy magazines...

On the verge of the Treaty on Basic Relations between Japan and
the Republic of Korea, our cultural autonomy is at risk of being
weakened by Japanese culture pouring in like a flood. (*The Chosun
Ilbo* 1963)

That "flood" continued to increase after the normalization of relations
in 1965. The importation of Japanese films was raised at the First
Japan–ROK Ministerial Meeting (*The JoongAng Ilbo* 1967b), and
while the Minister for Public Information Lee Chun-cheng stated, for
example: "We will allow the importation of Japanese cultural films, on
the condition that they are not exhibited to the general population"
(*The Chosun Ilbo* 1967), internationally acclaimed Japanese films
were publicly shown at the "Asian Film Festival" and similar events.
At the 1966 Asian Film Festival held in Seoul, films including *Danshun*
(Warm Spring), *Nippon Dorobō Monogatari* (Tale of Japanese Burglars)
were screened, and in 1968, similarly, "Frank Nagai sang a Japanese
hit song for the first time" (*The Asahi Shinbun* 1968) at the Asian Film
Festival; but inside South Korea these events were met with caution,
being seen as "reconnaissance troops for Japanese cinema landing
operations sent by the Japanese industry and the government" (*The
JoongAng Ilbo* 1969). In other words, while the South Korean public
vigorously consumed Japanese cultural products and the South Korean
government's attitude appears somewhat ambivalent, the Japanese
and South Korean governments and film industries encouraged the
import of Japanese films, and critical social discourses continued to
warn about the threats from this foreign culture.

Image 4.4:
The scene at the 1968
Asian Film Festival
(*The Asahi Shinbun* 1968)

The inflowing Japanese popular culture that the newspapers were problematizing spanned all genres, including novels, manga, popular songs, and anime. However, the trigger for newspaper criticism about Japanese anime was the 1970 airing of *Adventures of the Monkey King*, broadcast on KBS under the title *The Great Adventure of Sonogong*. This was the first Japanese work whose nationality was revealed by promotional press releases to the media with headlines such as "First Japanese-made film to be generally released in our country, a joint production by Mushi Production in Japan and Fuji Television Broadcasting Company", and "Technicolor manga film, *The Great Adventure of Sonogong*" (*The Kyunghyang Shinmun* 1970). Even while printing those headlines, the newspapers criticized the government's ambiguous position on Japanese imports, as evidenced by the quote below.

> This work is a purely Japanese-made film. In the beginning, KBS did not intend to reveal that this film was Japanese, but when it became an issue, it made the excuse that "*The Great Adventure of Sonogong* was a wholesome work for children, aimed at foreign export, with no whiff of Japan" ... This is a big problem in that currently, when the Ministry of Culture and Information does not permit even events for the screening of Japanese films, let alone their importation, for KBS – an organ under the umbrella of the Ministry of Culture and Information – to air anything Japanese is not only a contradiction of government policy, but it also opens the way for other private commercial broadcasters effectively to incorporate Japanese films from here forward. We must both

Image 4.5:
The Great Adventure of Sonogong,
criticized for being "made in Japan"
(*The Dong-A Ilbo* 1970)

protest that the state-run broadcaster should be spending our nationals' taxes to implant Japanese style even in children's minds; and criticize the authorities' ambiguous policy around television programs. (*The Dong-A Ilbo* 1970)

Moreover, the term "nationality unknown" was used by newspapers to denote works that had been produced in Japan, imported through a third country such as the U.S. and translated as being "made in South Korea", criticizing them as vulgar things that would harm children's emotions. However, information about their nationality differed from article to article. As of 1971, most of the anime broadcast from the three major broadcasters were Japanese: KBS, seven titles, including *Gigantor, The Adventures of Hutch the Honeybee*; TBC, seven titles, including *Golden Bat, Astro Boy*; and MBC, four titles, including *Leo, Prince of the Jungle*, and *Prince Planet*; but there were also some newspaper articles that pointed out that "the majority are American works, but as they underwent bonded processing in Japan, they were effectively Japanese" (*The Dong-A Ilbo* 1971).

Thus, the newspapers criticized the broadcast of Japanese anime on grounds such as: 1) the inundation of Japanese-made works, and bad influence on children; 2) the evil influence of vulgar popular culture; 3) the absence of domestic television anime products, et cetera. In the 1980s, as South Korea plunged into a mass-consumption society, the newspapers continued to criticize the ever-increasing amount of Japanese anime on television.

Today's leaders need to reflect deeply on the indiscriminate reception of Japanese culture, making South Korea like Japan. The responsibility of press institutions is heavy. From the beginning of the 1980s, imitation of Japanese broadcasting was a serious problem. Children's manga films such as *Big-eyed Frog, Candy Candy, Marine Boy, Astro Boy*, and *Tiger Mask* are all Japanese productions. (Broadcasting Deliberation 1986: 23)

This unrelenting attack on Japanese anime created a frame in which "children are always in contact with coarse and vulgar culture". Criticism of the circulation, plagiarizing and imitation of Japanese popular culture argued that it degraded the quality of domestic popular culture, which was being rapidly commercialized. For most of its history, the Republic of Korea had been governed by authoritarian dictatorships, and it was only in the 1990s that citizens' groups became active in South Korean society. It was only then that surveillance, indictment and criticism of the trans-bordering of Japanese culture really began. In retrospect, it is apparent that during the ban on Japanese culture in the 1970s, apart from the newspapers, there was hardly any explicit criticism of its inflow.

There is, however, a need for critical examination of the efficacy of the ban. In the first place, under the so-called "Yusin (restoration) regime" in October 1972, when Park Chung-hee assumed dictatorial powers, the 1970s were a period when the government only allowed criticism of an extremely limited range of issues. Newspapers were perhaps able to raise questions about the ban on Japanese popular culture and the government's ambiguous position because this was not a "political" issue so much as one of "popular culture." What might that mean? In a society in which the media did not function as a monitor of the government, ironically, newspaper criticism might have served to intensify public and private censorship of popular culture through social discourse. In sum, without acknowledging various contradictions inherent in that ban, the newspapers continued to call for a social awakening based on nationalism, and thus played a role in constructing the "mechanism of negation" by focusing solely upon the media commercialism and patterns of mass consumption of Japanese popular culture.

Intersection of the media industry and media discourse

Considering the airing of Japanese television anime in the context of the ban on Japanese popular culture, television might be seen as a "transgressive medium," and newspapers as a "censoring medium." But then we must ask why the newspapers' criticisms did not appear to influence the airing of Japanese anime. We must also note that the newspapers continued to publish reviews of new Japanese anime programs, even while criticizing their circulation and consumption.

These considerations problematize framing television as a "transgressive medium" and newspapers as a "censoring medium."

Let us return to 1971 to clarify this issue. The following article is critical of the airing of Japanese anime.

> Recently, low-quality manga have been removed, and new manga and manga films [=anime] have provided interest and awareness of issues; and anime fans have expanded to include the adult generation. TBC-TV's *Tiger Mask*, in particular, is liked more by adults than children. *Tiger Mask* is carried in *Sonyeon JoongAng*, also, and is widely read. (*The JoongAng Ilbo* 1971c)

The same newspaper published the following review in 1974.

> From August 1, the TBC Radio program, *Boys' Theater*, will broadcast a radio dramatization of the popular manga from *Sonyeon JoongAng*, *Shoot the Sun*. *Shoot the Sun* recreates the genius baseball player Jang Ung's tenacity and fighting spirit, and thrilling game scenes. (*The JoongAng Ilbo* 1974)

These two articles introducing programs – one on television, the other on the radio – share three similarities. First, the broadcaster in both cases was TBC; second, the manga versions of *Tiger Mask* and *Shoot the Sun* were both published in the boys' magazine *Sonyeon JoongAng*; and third, *JoongAng Ilbo*, the broadcaster, the newspaper and the magazine were all owned by the same parent company, the Samsung Group.

Image 4.6: Program introduction in *The JoongAng Ilbo* (left); supplement in *Sonyeon JoongAng* (center); cover of *Sonyeon JoongAng* (right)

Boys' magazines that were launched from the mid-1960s became an influential cultural medium in the 1970s. Among these, the most influential were *Saesonyeon* (launched 1964), *Sonyeon JoongAng* (1968), and *Eokkaedongmu* (1967), which were engaged in fierce competition. It would be no exaggeration to suggest that, apart from pirated versions, almost all Japanese manga was published by one of these three boys' magazines, using similar methods to those described for television anime; typically, either: 1) South Korean manga artists would do all the drawings, and attach their own names as the creators; or 2) unmodified copies of the original drawings would be attributed to fictitious South Korean manga artists.

> *Hurricane* [a supplement to *Sonyeon JoongAng*] was a standout among boxing manga. I never imagined it was a Japanese manga, but it was really entertaining... I cannot exclude the wrestling manga, *Tiger Mask*, similarly a supplement to *Sonyeon JoongAng*, which also was popular as an anime. Its content being what it was, oh, the pathos of its theme song that said: "The rain and wind blows again today from within the square jungle"! (Lee 2004: 78–79)

These South Korean "adaptations" of Japanese manga erased any so-called *waesaek* from the costumes and settings. As indicated in the Appendix, many Japanese manga were translated and distributed as South Korean products, mainly in boys' magazines and paperbacks as well, using the methods employed in "adapting" television anime. These processes were fully supported by the original Japanese publishers who, to avoid provoking anti-Japanese sentiment, made the appointment of local writers a condition of their licensing agreements (Natsume 2003: 181–182).

An editorial in *The Chosun Ilbo* criticized the circulation of Japanese manga as follows.

> It has become clear that 83.5 percent of manga are inferior. These manga are ones that have directly copied or translated Japanese manga such as samurai tales or decadent love stories. National measures are being demanded to control the situation in which

there is a flood of Japanese manga drawn by fictitious manga artists. (*The Chosun Ilbo* 1976)

But while the newspapers of the day were clearly fulfilling the journalistic roles of monitoring and criticizing the inflow of Japanese popular culture, it is hard to explain the roles of those newspapers and broadcasters simply as being complementary.

Behind all these phenomena lies the structure of composite media enterprises in 1970s South Korean society. The South Korean media industry at the time was characterized by the emergence of huge corporations concentrated in specific enterprises, and the cross-ownership of newspapers and broadcasting that stemmed from it. The Samsung Group, a composite corporation owning both *JoongAng Ilbo* and TBC (Tongyang Broadcasting) is a typical example of this. From the 1960s, Samsung acquired companies across three media: newspapers, television and radio. While this maneuver sprang from Samsung's own strategic planning, it was in complete accord with the government's political objective of establishing and exploiting a media production system that was friendly towards the regime. Furthermore, the ownership of broadcasting by financial conglomerates, media cross-ownership, and the criteria for reauthorization of ownership were not legally defined (Cho 1994; Park 1993).

Such a media industry structure did not fulfill the function of mutual inter-media critique. Instead, the media was used to strengthen and preserve their owners' market domination. This collapse into extreme commercialism was the most serious problem in the structure of the South Korean media industry in the 1970s.

The mainstream media of the day, including newspapers and television, while on the one hand monitoring and criticizing – in short, censoring – the permeation of Japanese popular culture in South Korea, on the other hand had strong economic interests in the Japanese popular culture in question. In other words, in a situation with no clearcut governance or regulation, the media assumed the extremely ambivalent position of simultaneously censoring the inflow of Japanese popular culture; and adapting and distributing it.

These contradictory roles of the media emerged directly from the ban on Japanese popular culture. In the absence of clearly legislated regulations, these contradictions served as a "mechanism of negation" which reinforced the ban even while violating it and censoring those violations. That is to say, both the state and the media maintained ambivalent attitudes, shuffling between decolonization and modernization.

The diffusion of pirated videos and Japanese popular culture

Mass consumption society and the Japan boom

The Chun Doo-hwan regime (1981–87) exercised extreme control over the cultural domain. The public broadcasting system – launched as part of the 1980 structural reorganization of the news media – effectively functioned as a medium for government control of public information. Heavy governmental suppression operated as a force to control media and popular culture in their entirety. The censorship maintained since the 1970s expanded, introducing legal measures related to public safety that had no direct connection with culture yet were exploited to suppress culture and the arts. However, it was also a period in which enormous amounts of capital were invested in cultural industries in response to the explosion in domestic demand (*The Ministry of Culture and Sports Report of South Korea* 1994: 81–82). In short, the cultural space during the Chun administration was shaped by two forces: political suppression by the government, and monopoly capitalism. In the 1980s, South Korea transformed into a mass consumption society through rapid economic growth. A commercial culture centered on mass production and mass consumption appeared along with new media, and in those circumstances, as we have seen, Japanese popular culture was consumed in various forms. Portable stereo cassette players such as the SONY Walkman gained popularity and, alongside new media such as videos and video games, prompted the spread of Japanese popular culture through pirated recordings. In contrast to the strict regulation and control of television broadcasting by the Broadcasting Ethics Committee and Korean Broadcasting Commission, it was effectively impossible to regulate these new media as the emerging middle class ravenously consumed these products. Videos and cassette tapes spread widely at the same time as teenagers joined the ranks of consumers along with their middle-class families (Kim 2003: 155).

The spread of video and audio, and reproductive media such as cassette tape recorders, had an enormous influence on the patterns of cultural consumption which, until the 1970s, had been insular, unidirectional and passive. In the 1980s, vendors of pirated tapes had become a common sight on the streets, an integral part of the urban space. The Recording Industry Association of South Korea reportedly uncovered 118 cases of unauthorized or illegal recordings in 1978 and 397 in 1979. In 1979 alone, more than 400,000 pirated versions of recordings had been seized (*The Chosun Ilbo* 1979; 1980). However, the "Copyright Act" and "Act Pertaining to Phonogram Recording" did not address these media, making it almost impossible to respond to this illegal recording. In the 1980s, a reform of the "Phonogram Act" strengthened policing of illegal recordings but it did not bring about effective change in the distribution or the market for phonogram recordings.[2]

Pirated recordings of Japanese popular music were extremely popular. The price of pirated recordings of Japanese hit songs (3,000 to 5,000 won) being sold on the streets at the time was up to ten times more than copies of American pop music (300 to 700 won) (*The Chosun Ilbo* 1984). Behind this was a boom in Japanese popular music, driven by young people, especially university and high-school students, not the older generations who had enjoyed singing Japanese popular songs at karaoke, the "Japanese language generation" who had been forced to use Japanese during the colonial period, or the post-independence "industrialized generation".

---

2 In South Korea, so-called "illegal recordings" were phonogram records that were copied and circulated without being produced by existing record companies or being deliberated by the Live Performance Ethics Committee. In the 1980s, according to cultural scholar Kim Chang-nam, there were two types of illegal recordings: the first was "illegally copied records" that were seen on the streets; while the second were "phonogram recordings of popular songs" that were produced in violation of political censorship (Kim 2003: 159–160). These two types of illegal recordings could be seen to symbolize the 1980s, when political control and consumerism co-existed.

In university districts such as Shinchon and Chungmu-ro and entertainment quarters, popular cafes played the latest hit songs by Kondō Masahiko, Saijō Hideki, Matsuda Seiko and the like (*The JoongAng Ilbo* 1986b). According to a survey in a monthly cinema magazine, *Screen*, of the fourteen music cafes in Seoul that the reporter visited, more than half were playing Japanese hits (*Screen* 1984a). This booming popularity was reflected in the market for pirated recordings, with the price of pirated cassette tapes rising almost 500%, from around 600 won to around 3,000 won. That boom can be interpreted as indicating a new trend in consumption culture. As shown in a 1985 newspaper article: "35 out of 60 in a class of female high-school students avidly read Japanese magazines" (*The JoongAng Ilbo* 1985a). Japanese media that was directly imported without translation or adaption informed young readers of new trends from overseas. Young people in their teens and twenties willingly accepted new Japanese cultural products, in full knowledge of their national origins.

However, the younger generation were not alone in the consumption of 1980s Japanese popular culture. While the younger generation was listening to Kondō Masahiko's *Gin gira gin ni sarinaku* (Flashy but cool) at music cafes, their parents' generation, who regarded the younger generation's new culture of consumption as problematic, was singing Ishida Ayumi's *Blue Light Yokohama* at karaoke. In spite of the military regime's announcement of "measures to ban the telecast of absurd fantasy anime," many anime were still being aired with their nationality hidden on television, which had begun broadcasting in color. These included *Mahō no yōsei Perusha* (Persia the Magic Fairy), *Kyandi Kyandi* (Candy Candy); *Mahō no purinsesu Minkī Momo* (Magical Princess Minky Momo) (Broadcasting Deliberation 1985). Meanwhile, newspapers continued to criticize the lively import and consumption of Japanese magazines such as *Bungei Shunjū* and *Shufu to Seikatsu*, and various fashion magazines targeting young people, like *non-no* and *an an* (*The JoongAng Ilbo* 1984c; *The Dong-A Ilbo* 1986). In short, as South Korea transformed into a consumer society in the 1980s, the consumption of Japanese popular culture was booming within the space of the long-running ban on Japanese popular culture.

The diffusion of pirated Japanese videos

The new problematic for the "ban on Japanese popular culture" in the 1980s was video. It was around 1980, when color television broadcasting was launched, that the medium called video was formally introduced to the market in South Korea. The starting-points were in 1979, when the first domestically-made video players were produced by major firms such as Daewoo, Samsung and Goldstar, and in September 1981, when five companies (Daehan Video Production, Saishin Image Public Corporation, Hankook Culture Image, Samhwa Video Production, Hankook Video Document Center) registered with the Ministry of Culture and Information and began video production, the reproduction and sales of theatre versions of films, and so forth. Until then, Japanese video players costing more than 900,000 won had been imported and distributed (*The Dong-A Ilbo* 1979a; *The Kyunghyang Shinmun* 1981a).

By the mid-1980s, with around 500,000 video players having been sold, social attention turned towards video. Film and video specialist magazines such as the monthly *Screen* (Korea) (launched March 1984) and the *Monthly Video* (April 1985) were launched in this period. However, the inaugural issue of the sole video specialist magazine, the *Monthly Video*, observed that contrary to early expectations, as video became more widespread, it began to be described as a "negative and decadent medium." Although *Monthly Video* pushed back, arguing: "From its outset, mistaken perceptions relating to video became widespread, ... and [people] immediately misconstrue videos as being something lurking like poisonous toadstools in a shady spot, to watch in some clandestine, secret place, almost imagining them to be low-quality, pornographic films" (*Monthly Video* 1985a). The market for pirated videos exploded, and sexual and violent movies inundated Korea through the copying and sales of foreign videos brought to Korea by U.S. military personnel and foreign tourists, as well as those produced by local video production companies (*Screen*, 1984b).

The normalization of videos as video players became common household appliances radically transformed the media and urban space, just as street televisions had in the 1960s. Television monitors were placed in restaurants and eating houses in Seoul's inner-city business and entertainment districts such as Myeongdong, Chungmuro and Namdaemun, of course, as well as cafes and the lounges of saunas, and these showed smuggled or pirated Japanese videos (*The Dong-A Ilbo* 1979b; *The Kyunghyang Shinmun* 1981b). The proliferation of pirated videos contributed significantly to negative perceptions vis-à-vis videos.

As with broadcast television, Japanese films and anime constituted the most desired content in South Korea's video industry, which grew rapidly with "production improvement as a strategic industry of the state, and creation of domestic demand," "overheated copyright competition over overseas film production companies in the process of opening-up" and "distribution of illegally copied videos in the early stages" (Jeon 1990: 68). There were cases of trans-bordering Japanese television broadcasts being recorded on videotape in Busan and circulated to other cities (*The Chosun Ilbo* 1981). The distribution of those videos transformed what had hitherto been a local experience of Japanese popular culture into one enjoyed across the nation.

> Japanese television programs that can be watched in Busan are exerting a huge influence on television in our country. Occasionally, programs with the same format as Japanese ones are aired, as well. Japanese televised variety shows that have been copied onto videotape also are making the rounds. Many copied versions of Japanese television programs are found at city-center video stores, which have been rapidly proliferating lately. Officially, the distribution of Japanese films, song records, videotapes and so forth in the South Korean market is forbidden at present. But the reality is different. Around fifty percent of merchandise at video stores is made up of Japanese-produced entertainment. Most of that consists of copied versions video-recorded down Busan way. (*The Dong-A Ilbo* 1981)

As mentioned previously, the Japanese origins of many popular anime which had been "adapted" for the Korean market began to be revealed due to video culture.

> Last month, at a sports carnival held at a certain private elementary school in Seoul, when one student started singing a cheer song in Japanese, numerous students joined in to sing the Japanese song

in unison, and not only the teachers, but also parents and others who had come to see the sports carnival, were aghast. The student in question sang the theme song from the Japanese anime *Mazinger Z* which they had seen on video at home, but, astonishingly, when they began to sing it, other students, too, joined in to sing it in its original language, and so a Japanese song suddenly rang out... Sixteen out of twenty [video] tapes of children's manga films on sale at S video store in an underground shopping arcade in Chung-gu in Seoul's Sogong-dong were Japanese-language versions often requested by children, such as *Marine Boy*, *Ujusonyeon Atom* (*Astro Boy*), and *Aladdin and the Magic Lamp*... B video store in Apgujeong in Seoul's Gangnam-gu, also, is equipped with space fantasy manga films for children that have been aired on Japanese television, including *Doksuri Ou-Hyungjae* (Eagle-5), *Mazinger Z* and *Robot Sigma*. (*The Chosun Ilbo*, 1981)

With this growing social attention, the merits of video began to be debated in earnest. In the mid-1980s, there were 400 shops hiring and selling videos in Seoul alone, and there were 33 video production companies, in contrast to the five which had existed in 1981 (*The Kyunghyang Shinmun* 1984); and throughout the 1980s, video-related magazines, as well as established newspapers, questioned the distribution and consumption of videos in the black market.

Monthly Video's editorial stance demonstrated that the problematization of Japanese videos was extremely ambivalent. From its launch, *Monthly Video* reported on the flood of Japanese video content, but at the same time, they happily reviewed and promoted Japanese videos to fill its pages. While criticizing the proliferation of Japanese anime videos, which accounted for ninety percent of anime, it simultaneously profiled Japanese anime in its "recommended video corner" and suchlike; and while exposing the smuggling and distribution of American and Japanese pornographic videos, it published profiles of Japanese adult videos and their female stars, including nude photographs.

In the situation where pornographic videotapes are reaching their heyday in Japan, the video kingdom, so-called "[adult] video actresses" are bathing in the limelight. Young women aged from their late teens to early twenties make their appearance in audacious poses, showing the style of the sex kingdom in an anticipated manner. (*The Monthly Video* 1986)

Moreover, as can be seen in Image 4.7, articles reporting on new developments in video hardware frequently reproduced Japanese images.

As such, videos were perceived as symbols of consumerism and hedonism as well as windows onto vulgar and decadent foreign cultures in the 1980s, a dilemma that many societies experienced as video technology became globally ubiquitous.

1. When video initially arrived, it was an expensive personal luxury affordable only by the wealthy, and black-market videotapes from overseas rapidly circulated.

2. As early-uptake video users were political and economic elites, it was not easy to regulate the reception of video by a minority from the start.

3. In those states beset by political confusion, the powerful often seek to distract the populace from politics by tacitly permitting the use of videos for entertainment.

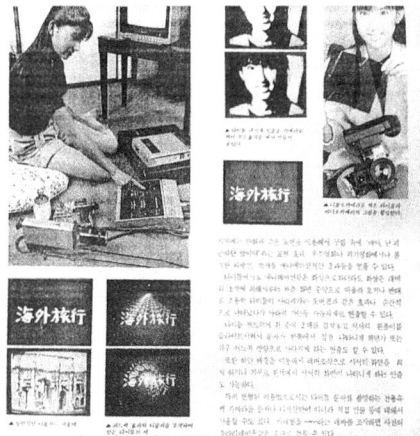

Image 4.7:
Articles on video editing published in *Monthly Video* which directly reproduce Japanese images (*Monthly Video* 1985b)

4. Thus, no mechanism is introduced for policing the circulation of illegal videos, nor for stringently censoring videotapes. (Jeon 1990: 63)

In this way, in the South Korean media space of the 1980s, when consumerism and hedonism proliferated, the distribution and consumption of Japanese popular culture by video continued to shape the ban while incorporating a negative perception of the role of pirated videos on South Korea's media culture. The signal spillover that had created Busan's media and urban space in the 1960s and 1970s spread to Seoul and across the nation through the new medium of video.

In the process, the urban space that was Seoul started to become a strongly liminal space, and the "mechanism of negation" that had sustained the ban on Japanese popular culture had to radically change. That is, the spread of video enabled more direct consumption of foreign culture, and Japanese popular culture came to be openly and directly consumed. The previous modes of trans-bordering via various kinds of distortion such as translation, adaptation and rearrangement were redundant, replaced with direct introduction. This meant that the "mechanism of negation" around the ban on Japanese popular culture ceased to operate. As the period of developmental dictatorship (1960s to 1980s) neared its conclusion, the ban on Japanese popular culture was beginning to be dismantled. In Part Three, we will look at the evolving modification of that "mechanism of negation."

Dismantling the Ban on Japanese Popular Culture

How was the "ban" dismantled? And how did the Japanese–South Korean cultural structure change with globalization in East Asia?

5

Chapter **5**

THE EXPANSION OF GLOBALIZATION AND SHIFTS IN THE BAN

With globalization, perceptions and attitudes towards Japanese popular culture changed from prohibition to liberalization. At the same time, the "mechanism of negation" in which consciousness and unconsciousness were blended in a complex manner also transitioned from a "collective consciousness" to "individual consciousnesses."

Reconstruction of the post-Cold War cultural map

Collapse of the Cold War system and awareness of the U.S.

In the late 1980s the international order established after the Second World War reached a turning point. As globalization penetrated national domains, nation-states around the world began restructuring (Sassen 2006). In South Korea, the military dictatorships and the developmental state spanning three decades were dismantled, as the processes of opening-up and democratization briskly unfolded in the late 1980s and early 1990s.

One important development in South Korea was a shift in consciousness and attitude towards American hegemony established through democratization and the collapse of the Cold War system. "Anti-U.S. consciousness" and Marxism, which hitherto had been prohibited, began to appear in various domains. The emergence of anti-U.S. sentiment in South Korean society was multi-faceted. Politically, it was a backlash against the U.S.'s tacit approval of the Chun Doo-hwan regime's violent suppression of the Gwangju Uprising. Economically, it was a revolt against U.S. pressure to open the country to globalized trade. Moreover, anti-U.S. sentiments spread in the democratization and opening-up phases of the late 1980s, bolstered by radical criticism of South Korea's political and economic dependence on the U.S. (Lee 2004: 248). In the late 1980s, with the collapse of the Cold War structure, questions began to be asked about the continuing presence of the U.S. garrisons, and anti-U.S. sentiment entered mainstream social discourse. The newspaper article below sums up the situation as follows.

> Recently, distrust and disbelief towards the U.S. which began to germinate on the momentum of the 1980 Gwangju Uprising have grown into an anti-U.S. logic by universities and opposition forces, and have transformed South Korean universities – in the "doldrums" in regard to anti-U.S. sentiment until now – into an anti-U.S. "typhoon belt"... Anti-U.S. sentiment, whose very discussion had been regarded as taboo until the 1970s in the "anti-U.S. = pro-communist" equation, began to spread fully to universities and ordinary nationals, with expectations towards the U.S., which they had believed would rein in South Korean armed forces at the time of the Gwangju Uprising, changing into a "sense of distrust". The discourse as to U.S. liability around the time of the Gwangju Uprising can be summarized into several claims, such as the U.S. having effectively allowed the commitment of troops by consenting to the lifting of operational control (OPCON) vis-à-vis the South Korean Army (20th Division), the refusal of an appeal from the Gwangju student leadership for mediation in a ceasefire, and its having supported government command of the armed forces. (*The Dong-A Ilbo* 1989)

In the media space, also, criticism and questions began to be raised around the American trans-bordering which had hitherto been unquestionably permitted. A prominent target of this critique was, needless to say, AFKN (U.S. military broadcasting), as discussed in detail in Chapter Two.

In 1988, South Korean researchers sought to resolve the question of AFKN's extraterritorial channel monopoly, which they saw as a critical challenge in reforming the broadcasting industry. This problematized AFKN's having

> continued for over thirty years to broadcast programs that match their state's advantage, convictions and ideas, in total ignorance of the country where it is stationed, based on the abstract and ambiguous content of the SOFA (Status of Forces Agreement) concluded in 1966 between South Korea and the U.S. (*The Chosun Ilbo* 1988)

The core of the issue was the use of VHF (Very High Frequency) channels. South Korean critics noted that:

> Even in respect of examples such as Japan or West Germany, where U.S. military broadcasts are using UHF (Ultra High Frequency) or cable television, there are no grounds for AFKN to use the limited VHF frequencies, particularly Channel 2, which has the most superior signal reception strength among them. (*The Hankyoreh* 1988a)

AFKN came to be seen as an obvious and immediate example of cultural imperialism (Tomlinson 1991), which had been raised in the 1970s by the United Nations, UNESCO and others, and had been debated for more than ten years before attention turned to AFKN, which had had a commanding influence on the South Korean media space for several decades.

This backlash against the U.S., which continued to push South Korea to open-up, was not the only factor behind this. Until then, South Korean society had remained rather secluded, even while enjoying the protection of its special relationship with the U.S. under the Cold War system. Thus, changing its relationship with AFKN, which had been its primary "window of contact" with other cultures, meant seeking new connections and cultural networks in a reorganizing global order.

South Korea progressively dismantled the various cultural practices that it had carried on with the U.S. as its ally since independence, which entailed fundamental changes in its relationship with, and perceptions and attitudes of, the U.S.

Even on an intellectual level, such a change appeared in material form in concert with the word "culture." Until the beginning of the 1980s, the concept of "culture" had not been an object of much consideration in South Korea. If one assumes that cities, science and technology, which had developed through modernization, as well as interest in popular culture and a critical consciousness vis-à-vis the hegemonic capitalism that dominated the social system, are necessary conditions for the introduction of cultural sociology (Smith 2001), then in the South Korean case, those conditions were only met in the late 1980s when it joined the global mass-consumption society, and when freedom of thought and diversity began to be guaranteed by democratization. In fact, it was not until the late 1980s that cultural sociology and cultural studies began to form as academic disciplines in South Korea (Kim 2014). Concerns about "America" were at the forefront of the introduction of "culture" as an academic area of interest. The new disciplines grasped cultural phenomena like cultural liberalization, the spread of consumerism, and the emergence of a new generation, while inheriting international theoretical developments from the 1960s and '70s when postmodern theories first emerged and the relationship between culture and society became a challenge; and becoming immediately immersed in the international developments of the 1990s, when global cultural discourses proliferated after the collapse of the Cold War system (Featherstone 1991). Domestically, in the democratization that followed the collapse of the Cold War structure, concepts and ideologies such as anti-Americanism and Marxism, which had hitherto been prohibited, became open objects of scholarship, along with new notions of culture.

Democratization and political censorship

The preface to Robert Goldstein's *Political Censorship of the Arts and the Press in Nineteenth-Century Europe* begins by describing South Korea in 1987, immediately after the collapse of the military dictatorship:

'The impact of works of art is so great that they can hardly be left with unlimited freedom', declared the South Korean Vice-Minister of Culture and Information, Choi Chang-yoon, in September 1987, amidst an election campaign widely viewed as presaging a liberalization of politics in that country. 'We have our social and moral values that must be defended and upheld', he added. 'We will not allow things brought up that are detrimental to our society or our national security'.

To prevent such 'detrimental' material from being distributed in South Korea, the government there traditionally has censored the press, books, movies, plays, songs and the visual arts, compiling a list of over 600 banned books and nearly 1000 forbidden songs by the 1987 election. Among the 186 songs which were released from the blacklist as part of the 1987 'liberalization' was one entitled 'Morning Dew' [*Achim Iseul*], an unofficial anthem of the student protest movement, which tells the story of a man who spends a painful, restless night, but then gains the courage to go on upon waking and seeing the dew. (Goldstein 1989: 1)

As Goldstein observed, following the collapse of dictatorial politics, South Korean society was finally attempting to escape from the violently suppressive rule of the 1960s to 80s, when freedom of expression and the press was restricted, and strict censorship applied to all kinds of culture. One part of this was an extensive reconsideration of cultural policy, symbolized by the "Ten-Year Master Plan for Cultural Development" announced in 1990 by the Roh Tae-woo administration. The Ten-Year Master Plan reinforced the Government Information Agency and made it independent of the Ministry of Culture and Information, while establishing a new Ministry of Culture. The GIA began to implement a cultural policy to promote and protect the culture industry, treating it as one avenue towards economic development. The 1994 founding of the Cultural Industry Bureau within the Ministry of Culture, and the addition of the concept of cultural industry to the Culture and Arts Promotion Act in 1995, both occurred in that context (Yeom 2008: 214).

One important development of the new cultural policy was to break away from the political censorship that had been consistently used by every form of government in South Korea since the colonial years. When mass media spread and the popular culture industry started to develop in the 1960s, censorship was carried out by numerous organizations, including the Motion Picture Ethics Committee, Broadcasting Ethics Committee and the Arts Ethics Committee, as well as by the legal system through the State Security Act, Assembly and Demonstration Act, and similar. This political censorship suppressed the rise of youth culture in the 1970s and gave rise to 1980s film culture in which only non-political and sexual expression were liberalized. It was a powerful force that determined the very shape of South Korean popular culture. Accordingly, the very first thing the government did in 1988 to demonstrate that its democratization would deliver real cultural change was to liberalize popular culture from the control of state censorship.

Of course, political censorship itself was deeply embedded in South Korean culture and was not easily dismantled. Indeed, there were several hurdles to overcome on the path to liberalization. Politically, the Roh Tae-woo military regime, imposed immediately after democratization, was in many ways limited in its ability to effect change to either the culture or the political structure. Economically, it would take time to transform the cultural industries that had developed and operated under strict cultural and social censorship, as well as the public's perceptions of popular culture.

Perhaps the most immediately visible change that democratization brought about was that political censorship – including ideologies and practices hitherto prohibited – came to be openly discussed in public. That is to say, the struggle over political censorship meant, on the one hand, demolishing the public censorship long enshrined in state cultural policy; and on the other, escaping from the self-censorship deeply embedded in private culture industries over several decades. Under these circumstances, the South Korean media space, restructured with democratization, had to free itself from deep-rooted prohibitions spanning all dimensions, including structures, systems, ideas and practices.

Opening-up and the East Asian cultural map

In September 1988, just after the Seoul Olympics, an incident arose in which two snakes appeared in the Korea Theater in Seoul's Myeong-dong district. Two film directors had carried the snakes into the cinema, which was showing the Hollywood movie, *Fatal Attraction*. They said they had done it to express their opposition to the direct delivery of Hollywood films by UIP, the overseas distributor of major U.S. film production companies. This incident symbolically represented the domestic industry's opposition to the opening of the cultural industries market, which in the late 1980s had been presented as an "irresistible tide of the times". For the popular culture business in South Korea, which had been descried as a "hermit kingdom" by the international news media until the mid-1980s, opening-up was an extremely shocking development that would shake domestic media cultural industries to their very core.

Of course, this was not only about the diffusion of global media, typified by Music Television (MTV), or the U.S.'s export-directed strategy. The various phenomena arising from opening-up were not confined to the simple question of whether to open up the domestic

Image 5.1: 1 January 1989 newspaper advertisements for films including *Empress Dowager Cixi* (China–Hong Kong co-production), *Die Hard* and *Rambo 3* (U.S.), *Moscow Does Not Believe in Tears* (U.S.S.R.), and *The Lie* (Italy) (*The Kyunghyang Shinmun* 1989)

market to foreign culture, but involved the reorganization of every domain in South Korea at the end of the so-called developmental state period, which was itself divided into a formation period (1960s), a solidification period (1970s), and a period of decay (1980s).

The cultural map that had prevailed in South Korea until then was re-drawn through this re-organization. Cultural policing – what had been dubbed "iron control" – was eased and hitherto prohibited cultural exchange with the communist bloc, such as the U.S.S.R and the People's Republic of China (P.R.C.), began around the time of the 1988 Seoul Olympics (*The Kyunghyang Shinmun* 1988). Its starting-point was the television broadcast of the Soviet film, *War and Peace* (1988) and the theatrical release of the China–Hong Kong joint production, *Empress Dowager Cixi*. The exhibition of American movies in cinemas – until then accounting for most foreign films – along with those from countries belonging to the communist bloc, was the most pointed expression of the cultural landscape of the late 1980s. Little by little, restraints were eased and cultural exchange with North Korea hitherto the target of a total "freeze," also began to be promoted. North Korean literature and arts were partially liberated amid mounting calls for consolidating the Korean Peninsula's contemporary cultural history. Significant developments included the full lifting of sanctions in July 1988 on "pre-independence literary works by [South Korean] writers abducted by or who emigrated to North Korea," the October "lifting of the ban on works of fine arts and music by artists abducted by or who emigrated to North Korea," and the lifting of sanctions on North Korean newspapers and books. These developments stimulated interest in North Korea. As part of a public campaign to "know North Korea properly," spearheaded by universities (*The Hankyoreh* 1988b), essays and books relating to North Korea started to be published from 1988, with magazines such as *Historical Review, Central Monthly*, and *Culture and Arts* publishing special features on North Korean history, thought and culture, and so forth.

In this social atmosphere, various developments in popular culture radically changed South Korea's cultural map, in concert with the rapid global shift towards a post-Cold War order. Notable among these changes was the rise of a new media space in South Korea, characterized by the proliferation of commercial culture and a new craze for Hong Kong cinema. The entire East Asian region had entered an age of mass consumption with a new and growing middle class of mass consumers enjoying cultural and economic opening and liberalization, and came to share a common media space through factors such as the spread of satellite broadcasting, the development of relevant laws, and the expansion of the market. These were unprecedented changes. Connected internationally by a trans-bordering network of commercial popular culture, the East Asian region took shape as an entity in the post-Cold War cultural map. Needless to say, the East Asian region in this new cultural map remained strongly connected to the U.S., while opening new connections with China and North Korea, and substantially redefined the systems and practices of domestic popular culture. Various mechanisms of prohibition regarding popular culture began to be dismantled in this reorganization. Moreover, moves to ease the rigorous control previously directed towards communist states further weakened the legitimacy of the ban on Japanese popular culture. In short, the "mechanism of prohibition" which had been integral to the Cold War structures rapidly disintegrated with the collapse of that order.

Reorganizing the legal system vis-à-vis the ban

Japanese popular culture in terms of copyright

In the context of advancing cultural globalization from the 1980s through the development of the substructures and institutions necessary for the production, transmission and reception of cultural products (Held, McGrew, Goldblatt and Perraton 1999: 370), the South Korean "ban on Japanese popular culture," also, was called into question. The state of the legal system and media practices relating to the inflow of Japanese popular culture, which had until then been "negated," were progressively thrown intro relief and problematized by globalization. Its axis was an insubstantial legal mechanism – one that relied upon regulation through permission from the Minister of Culture and Information based on presidential decree for the importation of foreign works – which lost its validity amid cultural globalization. This first came to a head through the contradictions around copyright.

Issues relating to copyright between Japan and South Korea gradually started to surface in the 1980s. In 1981, the publisher of the Japanese novel *Nan to naku, kurisutaru* (Somehow Crystal), Kawade Shobō Shinsha, protested the publication of pirated versions by four South Korean publishers (*The JoongAng Ilbo* 1981); and in 1984, the composer of Cho Yong-pil's hit song, *Return to Busan Port*, protested to the Japanese record company and JASRAC (Japanese Society for Rights of Authors, Composers and Publishers) about non-payment of royalties and so on. However, Japan and South Korea did not have any legal agreement in regard to creative works, as noted by a Japanese commentator: "As for the matter of royalties for 'Return to Busan Port', because no copyright agreement exists between Japan and South Korea, and royalties are not being paid in respect of Japanese tunes, either, we do not have to pay for [use] of South Korean tunes" (*The JoongAng Ilbo* 1984a). However, along with further moves for liberalization as the Seoul Olympics approached, and as Japan–South Korea cultural exchange progressed, the limits of unofficial importation had already been reached.

The United States and the Universal Copyright Convention

South Korean copyright law had not been amended since its creation in 1957 in a form modeled upon the 1899 Japanese Copyright Law. During that period, the sole law or ordinance relating to works by foreign nationals was contained in Article 46 of the Copyright Act, as follows (Jeon 1993: 106–108).

15. Copyright Act (January 28, 1957. Law no. 432), Article 46

(Copyright of foreign nationals): In regard to the copyright of foreign nationals, the stipulations of this Act shall apply, except in cases where there are special stipulations in a treaty. However, in cases where there are no stipulations in a treaty regarding copyright protection, the person or persons who first domestically published the work in question shall solely receive the protection of this Act. (*The Ministry of Culture and Information of South Korea* 1979: 640)

However, from the 1980 decision to hold the Olympic Games in Seoul, South Korea began to find its place in the global economy, and copyright surfaced as an issue that had to be resolved to rid Korea of its image as a haven for pirates.

> In 1988, the Olympics will be held in our country. Sporting events, along with all cultural events, will be held before the eyes of the whole world. To have it known by the world at that time that our country is a country of pirates that has not joined the World Intellectual Property Organization is something that should be rectified. (Republic of Korea National Parliament 1981)

It was, however, direct pressure from the U.S. that prompted real change in the legal system. In the 1980s, suffering under enormous budget and trade deficits, the new Reagan administration in the U.S. touted a recovery of the return-on-investment ratio for American industry and the preservation of its competitiveness in domestic and overseas markets as economic objectives. One of the principal strategies of so-called "Reaganomics" was intellectual property rights, including copyright. At the time, many Asian countries were situated outside the global network, and the U.S. government created favorable market conditions for itself by negotiating bilateral agreements with countries that had not signed up to international agreements.

A huge shift occurred in South Korean copyright law in 1984, often considered to be the peak of Reaganomics (Han 1994: 35). The U.S. government, which had detailed violations of intellectual property rights such as trademarks, patents and copyrights by South Korea at the First South Korea–U.S. Company Ownership Talks in 1983, used the Third South Korea–U.S. Economic Conference, the Eleventh Korea–U.S. Trade Ministers' Talks, Commerce Ministers' Talks and similar meetings in 1984 to aggressively demand liberalization of the service sector, such as finance, insurance and cinema, and implementation of measures to protect patents, trademarks and copyrights (*The JoongAng Ilbo* 1984b).

In October 1985, the Reagan government's announcement of a "Super 301" vis-à-vis South Korea's infringement of intellectual property rights was a decisive scenario. This "Super 301" was a symbolic clause in the U.S.'s trade-oriented approach to intellectual property rights. When this clause was invoked, the South Korean government was left with no alternative but to accept the U.S.'s demands. Ultimately, through trade negotiations, the South Korean government agreed with U.S. demands to: 1) introduce a copyright law reform bill for foreign nationals' copyright protection by April 1986; 2) enforce it from 1987 after legislative measures; and 3) sign the Universal Copyright Convention by 1988 (*The JoongAng Ilbo* 1985b).

In response, forty South Korean publishing companies held a "rally to oppose foreign nationals' copyright protection" and called for the government to refuse "to sign the Universal Copyright Convention in order to safeguard national advantage and the autonomy of national culture, and to impede cultural colonization" (*The JoongAng Ilbo* 1986a). However, despite the fierce domestic backlash, in August 1986, the South Korean government consented to: 1) sign the Universal Copyright Convention in September 1986; and 2) make it retroactive to 1977 in regard to the rights of U.S. works. On October 20, 1986, a Copyright Act Reform Bill whose main provisions were to protect works by foreign nationals was tabled by the government and referred to the Education and Information Committee on October 22.

"Amended Copyright Act" Article 3 (Works by foreign nationals)

1. Works by foreign nationals shall be protected by the conventions which our country has signed or entered.

2. Works by foreign nationals ordinarily resident in our country (including foreign corporate bodies which have their main office in our country. Hereafter in this Article, the Same) and works by foreign nationals first published in our country (including works published in our country within thirty days of their date of publication in a foreign country), shall be protected by this law, regardless of the stipulations in Paragraph One.

3. It shall be possible to restrict the protection by conventions and this Act even of works by foreign nationals protected

by the stipulations in Paragraphs One and Two in cases where the other party's country does not protect works by nationals of our country. (Republic of Korea National Parliament 1986)

The South Korean government's signing of the Universal Copyright Convention on 1 October 1987 was a turning point, after which works from other signatory countries were protected by South Korean law. Subsequently, South Korean cultural industries, which had experienced an unprecedented reorganization in response to the demands of a new global order, found themselves once again in a completely new environment – one in which they had to radically transform themselves once again.

Modifying the ban

The issue of copyright, which hitherto had been concerned only with the "public interest" (Foucault 1978: 23) of South Korean society, was fundamentally changed by the legal adoption of the Universal Copyright Convention. This had a huge influence on the ban on Japanese popular culture, as well, as will become clear from subsequent developments. One month after the conclusion of negotiations with the U.S., the European Community and Japan demanded the same level of market access and protection of intellectual property rights as the U.S. (*The JoongAng Ilbo* 1987). Korea's signing of the Universal Copyright Convention was seen as an opportunity by the government and culture industries in Japan, as well. Akutagawa Yasushi, Director of JASRAC (Japanese Society for Rights of Authors, Composers and Publishers), attended the Japanese National Assembly in 1988, where he spoke about copyright in South Korea.

Regions in Asia where copyright management activities are undertaken are Hong Kong and South Korea, but a new Copyright Act was enforced in South Korea in July last year, and it also entered into the Universal Copyright Convention. As the Universal Copyright Convention does not apply retrospectively, although the levying of usage fees in regard to works performed by Japanese from

1 October onwards should naturally be implemented, as you know, in South Korea there is a ban on the performance of Japanese music via broadcasts or in ordinary live performances. Moreover, in light of the fact that [Japan] is a neighboring country, as a completely abnormal situation is continuing from the point of view of expanding cordial relations [between Japan and South Korea], we hope strongly that in such a matter as this, too, such restraint will soon be lifted somehow by political agency. (Japanese National Diet 1988)

Print publishing was the field in which the concrete effects of the new copyright law on the ban on Japanese popular culture first appeared. After the new laws came into effect, the legal importation of Japanese publications began. In 1989, Japanese manga including *Sangokushi* (Romance of the Three Kingdoms) and *Hokuto no Ken* (Fist of the North Star) were published or serialized under the first copyright contracts (South Korean Publication Ethics Committee 1990: 9–10). Also in 1991, "pre-screening" was introduced by the South Korean Publication Ethics Committee, which stated: "pre-screening should be implemented vis-à-vis manga whose translation and publication is effected by legal copyright contracts" (South Korean Publication Ethics Committee 1991: 46), and the sale of forty-five legally imported Japanese manga from three genres was permitted. This means that the formal importation of Japanese manga was carried out by means of formal contracts and pre-screening. Thus, almost a decade before the official announcement of the liberalization of Japanese popular culture, a partial dismantling of the ban had already begun within the media industries and the law. As stated in the following article, having signed the Universal Copyright Convention, South Korea had no choice but to systematize imports to avoid illegal sales of Japanese manga, and the international friction that would stem from it.

Such a decision [i.e., the enforcement of pre-screening] by the "South Korea Publication Ethics Committee" was one that arose from the judgement that some manga publishers were provoking serious problems, having jumped on the bandwagon of the recent publication liberalization policy to indiscriminately copy and publish obscene and violent manga from foreign countries such as Japan, and were not only exerting a bad influence upon the spirits of young people, but also were the cause of copyright disputes with foreign countries. (*The JoongAng Ilbo* 1991a)

In 1992, *Dragon Ball* was published through a formal copyright contract between the Japanese publisher Shueisha and Seoul Munhwasa. Around the same time, in response to the Broadcasting Act amendments of 1991, the Broadcasting Committee deliberated television anime and broadcast programs from overseas from July 1, 1992 (South Korean Broadcasting Committee 1992). Although the ban on Japanese popular culture was officially maintained, with the South Korean government rejecting Japanese demands for a cultural agreement (*The JoongAng Ilbo* 1992a), in effect, the ban was already beginning to be partially removed. For Japan the export of such manga, in line with the Universal Copyright Convention, meant their full-blown launch of manga and anime into the Asian market.

The Universal Copyright Convention's coming into effect thus began to govern cultural trans-bordering from Japan to Korea, not as a problem only involving those two countries, but in line with global standards. Of course, when "Japan as historical memory" is taken into account, it is not possible to reduce these changes to a simplistic schema, but there is little doubt that this global legal system substantively changed local practices. In other words, with the introduction of international copyright law, the mechanisms of "prohibition" and "trans-bordering", formed and maintained through historical circumstances, were dramatically impacted by the global order. It would be going too far to say that the ban was totally dismantled by the copyright issue, though. For example, the pre-screening program introduced in 1991 was discontinued after one month due to "national sentiment" and "market confusion." Hence, it would be more accurate to say that following the signing of the Universal Copyright Convention, the fierce conflict between the existing prohibition and the new liberalization intensified.

The system of pre-screening for foreign manga which [we] introduced in order to prevent the distribution of unwholesome foreign manga, and to accept wholesome and beneficial manga on the dimension of international cultural circulation of translated books, was mistaken by many manga publishers to represent the liberalization of Japanese manga; and from among Japanese manga with low manuscript fees and high profitability in comparison with domestic ones, there arose moves to publish those that had been issued prior to 1 October 1987, when there had been no necessity for a copyright contract, but this was immediately interrupted. (Publication Ethics Committee 2000: 26–27)

However, if one understands the ban on Japanese popular culture to be a complex manifestation of the legal system, media practices and social discourse, then through a change in the legal system, the local specificity – the historical memory of Japan which had hitherto enabled the ban – lost its validity as a ground for public policy in the context of the global order, which had a huge impact on the ban on Japanese popular culture. In fact, immediately after signing the Universal Copyright Convention, the South Korean government had to implement substantive import measures relating to Japanese manga and television anime because, despite robust feelings of resistance to lifting the ban on Japanese popular culture that lingered in South Korean society, it had to comply with the new norm defined by the Universal Copyright Convention. In other words, the issue of international copyright law in the 1980s brought local sentiments and practices generated by the historical context of Japan–South Korea relations into conflict with the new global norm introduced to South Korea by the U.S. In the end, the mechanisms comprising the ban on Japanese popular culture and discourse began to be dismantled through the conflict which that globalization provoked.

As discussed above, circumstances in the South Korean media space from the 1980s significantly complicated the ban on Japanese popular culture. It is important, however, to recognize that the dividing line between what was banned and what was permitted had already blurred with the lifting of the embargo on hitherto-prohibited culture from the communist bloc, and the limited application of a new legal system. However, in order to fully appreciate how the ban on Japanese popular culture was finally dismantled, we must examine how the three fields – the legal system, media practices and social discourse – that manifested the ban on Japanese popular culture changed in concrete terms, not merely as a change in policy.

New developments relating to Japanese popular culture

Japanese popular culture in live telecast

The growing audience for Japanese satellite broadcasting was a critical factor in dismantling the ban on Japanese popular culture. After formal permission was granted to import parabola antennas in January 1989, there was a rapid increase in the number of households directly viewing NHK1 and NHK2 via Japanese satellite broadcasting. By 1990, already, more than 200,000 households had begun watching Japanese television programs via satellite transmissions. Commenting on this boom in viewing Japanese satellite broadcasts, the South Korean Ministry of Culture stated: "As it is a natural phenomenon, we do not intend to regulate it" (*The JoongAng Ilbo* 1991b), but in fact, there was no legal criteria to police the installation of satellite antennas so as to sustain the ban on Japanese popular culture. In fact, when the Ministry of Foreign Affairs appealed to the Japanese government to prevent the penetration of Japanese broadcasting, the Japanese reportedly replied: "There are no grounds for its legal regulation" (*The JoongAng Ilbo* 1990).

This example of satellite broadcasting is typical of difficulties South Korean society faced in satisfying its lingering desire to prohibit Japanese popular culture which was by this stage inflowing via formal routes and in the context of rapidly advancing cultural liberalization. These difficulties were compounded by structural changes in cultural industries across the whole of Asia that could not be addressed bilaterally by Japan and South Korea alone. The inflow of Japanese popular culture had become an issue of East Asian globalization, as Japanese cultural commodities, starting with television dramas, were already widely popular in Hong Kong, Taiwan, China, and South-East Asian countries with Chinese communities (Shiraishi 2007; Hu 2003). The live television broadcast in 1988 of singing in the Japanese language is symbolic of the atmosphere at the time. At the "30 Days Before the

Olympics Festival", the Japanese pop group, Shōjōtai, sang the lyrics to the Olympic theme song, "Korea," for about one minute in Japanese, rather than the original English. This event was reported by the news media in both Korea and Japan.

> This scene was telecast live on television throughout South Korea. Having been colonized by Japan, but now rapidly internationalizing on the impetus of the Olympics, South Korea views the singing in public of songs in Japanese as "cultural invasion" and does not allow it. This is seen to have been the first incidence of a song in Japanese riding the radio waves... Japanese singers who have visited South Korea hitherto have sung in English or other languages at the request of the organizers. On September 10, immediately prior to the Olympics, Sugawara Yōichi, who traveled from Japan to appear in the Seoul International Song Festival, was also refused permission to sing in Japanese. On 8th, Shōjōtai, also, reportedly was requested beforehand "not to sing in Japanese."
> (*The Asahi Shinbun* 1988)

Shōjōtai recorded a cover version of "Korea", originally sung by Leslie Mandoki and Eva Sun, and also released it as a Japanese language single in Japan; and at the time, Shōjōtai's album of songs recorded in English was being formally sold through Seoul Records in South Korea. That minute at the pre-Olympics festival was reported under

Image 5.2:
A scene in which Shōjōtai sang a Japanese song in Korea
(*The Asahi Shinbun* 1988)

the headline "Japanese popular culture hurries to land in South Korea" (*The Hankyoreh* 1988c); and was described as the first performance of a Japanese song on television since independence. The fact that a record album by Japanese singers, albeit an English version, was being formally sold had hardly attracted attention until then.

However, the sale of Shōjōtai's album was extremely exceptional. This was because, in accordance with the deliberated stipulations of the Performance Ethics Committee until the mid-1990s, what was banned in South Korea at the time was the importation of "songs that Japanese people sang, naturally, but also those whose lyrics and music were composed by Japanese." In fact, in 1995 album, *Life until Deaf*, by the Japanese rock band "OUTRAGE" was released through Warner Bros. Korea, but even though all of the songs were sung in English, the album was identified as the product of a Japanese rock band, and was recalled. In other words, amid the diversification of routes and ways of inflow that accompanied liberalization, it was extremely difficult to establish criteria for the "ban" and ways to apply it. This will be obvious also from the way things seesawed: while live performances of Japanese songs were held in 1990 by Katō Tokiko and in 1993 by Kye Eun-sook, a live performance by the band Cassiopeia was disallowed in 1993 but then permitted in 1996 (*The Hankyoreh* 1996).

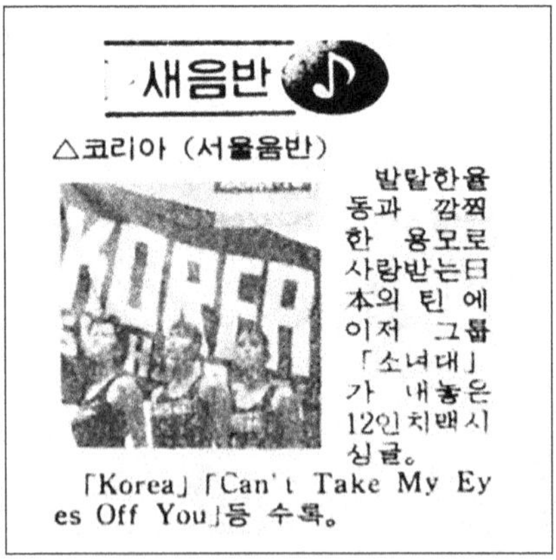
새음반

△코리아 (서울음반)

발랄한율동과 깜찍한 용모로 사랑받는日本의 틴 에이저 그룹「소녀대」가 내놓은 12인치팬시싱글。
「Korea」「Can't Take My Eyes Off You」등 수록。

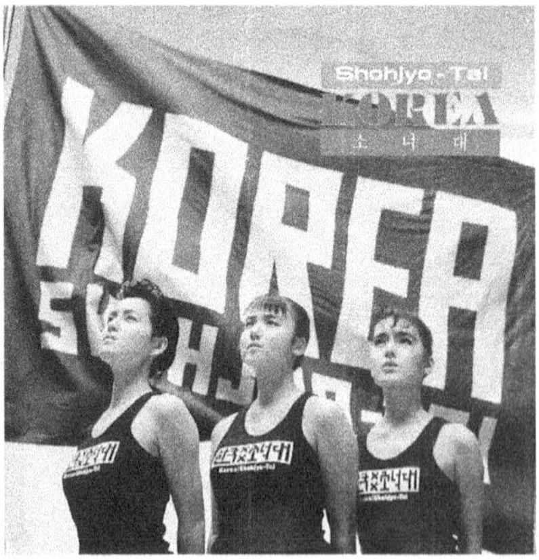

Image 5.3: At right is Shōjōtai's South Korean LP record; at left is a newspaper article introducing Shōjōtai's album: "The album released by the Japanese teenage group, 'Shōjōtai', beloved for their lively dancing and cute appearance" (*The Mainichi Shinbun* 1988)

In other words, from the point in the late 1980s when Shōjōtai's album was launched, while much of Japanese popular culture was still secretly trans-bordering, some of it began to be introduced through official media. The ban on content was being maintained, but in the course of opening-up, it was not possible to explicitly forbid interest in it. The point that deserves attention is that while the majority of the actual audience at live performances in Japanese by Kato Tokiko and Kye Eun-sook consisted of Japanese people living in South Korea, the recipients of music by Shōnentai, Kondō Masahiko, Matsuda Seiko and others comprised the South Korean younger generation. In short, at that point in time, already a certain degree of fandom had begun to be formed.

The November 1989 issue of the South Korean edition of *Roadshow*, for example, carried an interview with the chief editor of *Kinema Junpō*,

Image 5.4:
"1980s Japanese films now"
(*Roadshow* 1989)

Image 5.5:
Article entitled: "From the streets to living rooms…
[On] the scene of '*waesaek*'".
From left, satellite antennas, *waesaek* fashion, Japanese-language signboards, pachinko
(*The Dong-A Ilbo* 1991c)

131

Uegusa Nobukazu, entitled "1980s Japanese films, now." The article begins with the words: "There are probably no films as close to and distant from us as Japanese cinema."

> Japanese popular culture is inundating us. Fashion that is trendy in Japan is arrayed in Seoul shops in a week's time, and Japanese popular songs with incomprehensible lyrics are in vogue among our youth. (*The Dong-A Ilbo* 1991a)

Thus, in the late 1980s, the signal spillover that had defined the media space in Busan for decades had spread across South Korea as the society became increasingly open to the outside world. All kinds of Japanese popular culture was being consumed in the Japanese language through satellite broadcasting and literary magazines, as well as manga, films, fashion magazines, and pirated videos.

Media change under question

Japanese popular culture, which had trans-bordered in various ways since the 1980s, triggered a re-examination of the South Korean media, which was expressed as apprehension and a sense of crisis at the arrival of globalization, which had ushered in an opening of the media space.

In March 1990, at the fourth working-level consultations on Japan–ROK cultural exchange, the South Korean delegation broached the issue of Japanese satellite broadcasts being viewed by in excess of 200,000 households, pointed out cultural issues arising from the permeation of Japanese television broadcasting, and suggested that the Japanese make efforts to prevent that permeation and that the two countries should confer as to broadcast content. In response, the Japanese delegation, assuming the satellite broadcasting to be in compliance with the International Telecommunication Convention, an international treaty, apparently did not accept the suggestion, declaring that debating the content of broadcasting would be a violation of freedom of expression, and that the primary objective of satellite broadcasting was to reach Japanese areas with poor signal reception (Telecommunications Development Research Institute 1990).

As we can see, the signal spillover of Japanese television to more than 200,000 households could not be prevented without violating various international telecommunications agreements. As we saw in examining the issue of copyright, the bordering mechanisms that – although somewhat vaguely – had been maintained for decades had ceased to function in this period. These circumstances seemed to demand a radical reform of South Korean broadcasting. One of the most critical challenges to such reform would be the production practices of imitation and plagiarism of Japanese broadcasting which had hitherto been the norm.

> There is also a lot of diffusion of "*waesaek*" through domestic television. Many of the costumes and hairstyles of singers appearing on television shows are modelled directly on those of Japanese entertainers. Certain performers exactly mimic the Japanese way of speaking. Such "aping of Japan" by popular entertainers has an influence upon viewers, and *waesaek* is in vogue in ordinary people's hairstyles, fashion, dancing and so on. Moreover, the better part of variety program formats are those imitating Japanese programs, and the appearance of Japanese footwear – wooden "*geta*" – and uniquely Japanese musical instruments in such anime aired on domestic television as *Galaxy Express 999* and *Space Pirate Captain Harlock* reflect a Japanese atmosphere. (*The Dong-A Ilbo* 1990)

Especially amid the heated competition for audience ratings between the three broadcasters following the station launch in 1990 of SBS (Seoul Broadcasting System), the practices of imitating and plagiarizing Japanese television dramas, variety shows, and anime had reached a blatant level. In 1993 alone, Japanese programs such as *Fūn! Takeshi-jō* (Takeshi's Castle), *NHK nodo jiman* (NHK's Proud of My Voice), *Sekai marugoto HOW matchi* (How Much for the Whole World?), *Hyakuman-en kuizu hantā* (Million Yen Quiz Hunter), and *Tokyo Love Story* were "adapted" by South Korea television stations (*The Yomiuri Shinbun* 1993). Of course, these practices were not problems limited to television broadcasting, but rather, ran through the entire discourse on popular culture in South Korea in the context of globalization, as described by film critic Yang Young-mo below.

> Japanese films are landing in the Korean Peninsula. On the current of "globalization," the age of unconditionally excluding them due to hostility towards Japan has already passed. Rather, what is being sought is to depart from such an emotional perspective, to respond to and critique Japan and Japanese cinema properly in our own field of vision from a rational and realistic perspective, and to resolve the issues of Japanese style in our films, the misappropriation of Japanese works, and cinematic sensibility. (Film critic Yang Young-mo, *Screen* 1988)

Moreover, in 1991, the anime *Akira* was imported as the Hong Kong-made adaptation of *Hurricane Boy*, but when its Japanese origins became public knowledge after a week of screening in theatres, it was withdrawn as a matter of course, and the importer's registration was cancelled. Growing awareness of issues such as "nationality switching" since *Mazinger Z* began to cast doubt on the meaning and efficacy of the ban on Japanese popular culture. Building public pressure led to an argument for abolishing the Performance Ethics Committee. Various expedients and misshapen inflow patterns such as with the screening of *Akira* could be reproduced under a censorship system where there were ambiguous criteria and prior deliberation, namely: "Permission will be given to the importation solely of television anime, on the condition that they are not too laden with Japanese style; but their theatrical exhibition will be prohibited" (*The Dong-A Ilbo* 1991b).

Another important distortion to the inflow pattern was the market for pirated versions. In the case of Japanese manga, especially, pirated versions accounted for an overwhelming proportion of the market. According to a 1990 survey by the Publication Ethics Committee, 200 Japanese manga were produced by thirty-four publishing companies from 1987 to October 1990, but of these, 196 were unauthorized reproductions, that is, pirated versions (South Korean Publication Ethics Committee 1990). Another survey found that ninety-five percent of the 1500 manga published from 1991 to August 1993 were pirated versions (*The JoongAng Ilbo* 1993). Under these circumstances, questions began to be asked not merely about those who were producing, distributing and consuming these pirated versions, but also about ambiguities in the legal system and the government's position. It became clear that the market for pirated versions had been able to continue expanding due to the dilemma of trying to maintain a ban in a situation where formal importation had to be permitted.

> The Constitution of the Republic of Korea [1987] guarantees freedom of publication and speech. The concluding of formal copyright contracts with the original authors of foreign books, also, and the translation and publication of the same, are legal activities guaranteed by the Constitution. As they are undeniably publications, manga, too, are eligible for this treatment. In the case of Japanese manga, as well, if they are translated and published upon the conclusion of contracts for formal publication rights with their original Japanese authors, then they will be legal publications not legally subjectable to any restraint. Despite that, [the government] restricts such Japanese manga as being illegal, and will not even allow discussion... *In other words, [we are] in the curious dilemma whereby reproductions of Japanese manga circulating in the community are simultaneously both legal and illegal.* (Ministry of Culture and Sports 1994: 179, emphasis added)

The question "What does *waesaek* mean?", which is of course the starting point of the ban on Japanese popular culture, began to be discussed more broadly as well. A typical example was the dispute over whether the so-called "trot" (*teuroteu*) music of 1990 was "*waesaek*" or not. Trot is a genre analogous to Japanese *enka* (popular ballads), and its origins were always controversial, due to their similarities. The dispute over whether trot songs are "traditional songs or Japanese-style songs?" (*The Kyunghyang Shinmun* 1990) coincided with the 1987 lifting of the ban on *waesaek* tunes, which brought more social attention to questions of Japanese style. In the ambiguous situation in which Japanese satellite broadcasting was trans-bordering, and the dominance of Japanese style was a matter of concern in the market for manga and anime, it was probably a matter of course that the question "What constitutes *waesaek*?" would gain currency. However, as the non-resolution of the "trot dispute" demonstrates, there were no easy answers. Especially in circumstances where consumption patterns and cultural ideas about popular culture were opening to globalized media, as long as they did not directly represent Japanese imperialism from the colonial period, it was hard to differentiate *waesaek* from fashion.

Those were the circumstances behind a very interesting round-table discussion printed in the November 1987 issue of the monthly magazine, *Broadcast Culture* ("Roundtable discussion on TV anime"). The roundtable discussion, involving Kim Young-min, a producer in the MBC Television Production Department, Chung Wook, President of Daiwon Media Co., Choi Bong-nam, a producer in the KBS Film Department, and Lee Won-bok, a manga artist and a professor at Duksung Women's University, was held immediately after the airing at long last of South Korea's first domestically made television anime, *Wandering Magpie*. While pointing out that South Korean television anime skills were excellent – having been honed by the outsourcing structure over several decades – participants agreed that "their form only had well-developed lower bodies, without a head." The participants nevertheless expressed an expectation that the process of attaching a head had begun through that first anime work, *Wandering Magpie*. Chung Wook, President of Daiwon Media, which had created *Wandering Magpie*, described the state of South Korean television anime.

> Things are often pointed out as being "*waesaek*", but there are no criteria for judging "what, then, constitutes South Korean style?" We must hurry to accomplish its development and estab-lishment... American television anime are mainly short-form seven- or ten-minute cartoons based on gags. In order to catch up to the U.S., Japan developed television anime focused on content in a dramatized format. In our case, we still have no specific mode. Would it be better to see ours as a mixture? Imitation leads to creation, so I think that in time our own [anime] will come into being... In the technical aspect, the springboard for our leap onto the world [stage] is already in place, ... because most of the works that are popular in Japan and America are ones produced in our country... The question, though, is whether our design can catch up.

Here, Chung displays a far more positive view than many critics, notably scholars and journalists of the local industry's capacity to dismantle the decades-old production structure in a way that would promote its development. He also described the imitation of Japanese and American works as a process in which culture takes shape and grows, and turned his eye to the question of how Korea would be able to catch up with more advanced societies and then surpass them. To this end, he is less concerned with what constitutes *waesaek* than with what constitutes South Korean style and expresses his confidence that "our own [anime] will come into being." The perceptions and attitudes of the producers cannot be understood separately to the process of dismantling the ban on Japanese popular culture. In terms of the "mechanism of negation" that operated until then, if the imitation of Japanese television, films and popular music were a way of fulfilling the prohibition by disguising their Japanese origins, and if practice was a stratagem by the cultural industries of an emergent nation, then the widespread industry practices of imitation, plagiarism and piracy can be seen to have been direct products of the ban on Japanese popular culture itself.

Oddly, however, there had been relatively little interest in what constitutes South Korean style in the pursuit of the ban on Japanese popular culture, which had focused almost exclusively on decolonization. Was it perchance that having focused too much on the negatives – prohibition, exclusion – there had been too little attention given to the positive action of "creating"? Did the absence of positive intentions to create perhaps contribute to fulfilling the "negation"?

In other words, in terms of the ban on Japanese popular culture, the above comments could be seen as marking a huge change in thinking about the history of popular culture in South Korea by interrogating "Korean style" in light of the influence of U.S. and Japanese cultural industries on South Korean cultural industries, and a path away from the existing practice of "imitation." This perspective recognizes that the ultimate objective of decolonization is not simply to exclude the Other, but to have an equal relationship with the Other as an independent agent. Chung Wook was an interested party from an industry that was deeply engaged in earlier practices of imitation, but his experience on the ground gave him a perspective not available to those intellectuals who continued to champion "prohibition" based on a discourse of cultural imperialism. Soon thereafter, the first official South Korean report that addressed popular culture as an industry and policy was released, the 1989 *Study on the Popular Culture Industry and Popular Culture Policy* (Research Center for Cultural Development 1989), which indicates the enormous significance of this period as a turning point. In short, faced with the total reorganization of the media space, South Korean society began to acknowledge contradictions in the prevailing "mechanism of negation" and treat them as new industrial and cultural problems, not as a policy without a policy that presupposed the need for excluding Japanese popular culture.

From prohibition to liberalization

Under the new conditions of globalization, the practices of imitation became an issue for South Korea's cultural industries and reframed the ban on Japanese popular culture. In the late 1980s, as the frame of South Korean social debate about Japanese popular culture rapidly transitioned from prohibition to liberalization, the government's attitude to Japan changed, too, beginning to emphasize the close connection between Japan and South Korea as fellow travelers, against the background of a potent sense of anxiety and impending crisis over globalization.

Two newspaper editorials published in late January 1990 clearly express this anxiety. The first, titled "The U.S. is pressing," predicted that the preliminary ruling by the U.S. Department of Commerce's investigation of the dumping of South Korean-made steel products would lead to increased trade pressure from the new Clinton administration. The other, titled "Foreign rip-offs on television," discussed the problems with domestic production practices that plagiarized or copied foreign programs.

> It is common knowledge that domestic television broadcasting imitates foreign television programs. It has been a longstanding practice, timed with the twice-yearly programming revision period, to view foreign television programs, starting with those from Japan, and to copy or gain ideas about format from them and so forth...

138

The plagiarism of foreign programs by our television [industry] must be of concern not only to broadcasting professionals, but also jointly to our society. In the age of internationalization and opening-up, we must be a people accustomed to an international sensibility. However, it would be impossible for us to become autonomous international citizens merely by mimicking foreign culture. (*The Chosun Ilbo* 1993)

The uneasiness and sense of crisis exhibited here stemmed from acknowledging that the various media industry practices which had characterized the industry for decades would no longer be acceptable in the new order. In terms of the ban on Japanese popular culture, the bilateral Japan-South Korea frame which had long supported prohibition gave way to a global frame which prioritized liberalization. Assuming that practices such as plagiarism and imitation had been tacitly approved for the purpose of upholding the ban on Japanese popular culture, then dismantling the systems constructed for prohibition was now required, to comply with demands of the new, liberalized, global order. Of course, various forces and mechanisms of prohibition did not simply or instantly disappear in response to the powerful current of opening-up. The various systems, practices and discourses of rampant plagiarism and copying in all genres of popular culture – starting with popular music, and including films, broadcasting, manga, and novels – had not developed simply in response to the pressures for liberalization, but were also strongly shaped by the demands for prohibition at the same time. These tensions appeared markedly in discourses on the ban on Japanese popular culture. The principle that "South Korean national identity should be protected by banning Japanese popular culture" gave way to a new "discourse of protection" which argued that "South Korea's cultural industries should be protected by liberalizing Japanese popular culture." Clearly, what has changed most starkly is the "object that should be protected." Whereas "national identity" was the core object of protection in the discourses on the ban on Japanese popular culture until the late 1980s, "cultural industries" became the keyword in the prohibition discourse.

In that context, the South Korean government's shift towards the liberalization of Japanese popular culture was further strengthened by the Kim Young-sam regime, which touted "globalization" as its administration's catchphrase. A report published by the Ministry of Culture and Sports in July 1994, *Study on the Plan for Response to Japanese Popular Culture* (The Ministry of Culture and Sports 1994), in particular, shows that at this point in time, the policy to liberalize Japanese popular culture had effectively already been decided. According to this report, a master plan was proposed for an "experiment in phased liberalization from 1995" and for "full liberalization from 1998." There is also clear evidence that by 1994, public opinion had also changed significantly, with the number of people approving "liberalization" exceeding those opposing it.

Social debate began to refocus on a "reality principle" which accepted that Japanese popular culture was already flowing in and was widely consumed. Both those who favored liberalization and those opposed to it turned their attention to the question of "how to liberalize without harming domestic industry." As can be seen also from the following report, opening-up from the late 1980s forced understanding of the ban on Japanese popular culture to shift from a frame of bilateral relations to one of international relations; and it made public all kinds of "realities" relating to Japanese popular culture.

> In international relations, it is necessary to consider both non-discrimination and reciprocity. For example, our Film Division does not have the power of persuasion in international society to apply different criteria solely to Japan, even though we are hugely

Table 5.1: Surveys of public attitude towards liberalization 1992–'94

date	Survey institute	Approve	Reject
January 1992	Korea Opinion Institute	19%	79%
October 1992	Korea Broadcasting System	21%	78%
January 1994	Broadcasting Development Institute	52.3%	33.3%
February 1994	*The JoongAng Ilbo*	54%	37.5%
April 1994	National assembly, specialists	46%	53.5%

Source: Korea Cultural Policy Development Institute 1994: 139

encroached upon by the U.S. (The Ministry of Culture and Sports 1994: 208)

In other words, separately from the "reality" in which Japanese popular culture had been widely consumed until then, social consciousness vis-à-vis the ban on Japanese popular culture whose fulfilment had been vital was progressively dismantled. Acknowledgement of this was connected to the level of policy. The report examined the question: "What kind of procedures should we use to liberalize?" In recognition that opening-up to the popular culture of South Korea's most active partner in international exchange was an "inescapable trend of the times," the report proposed the following basic principles and items for consideration.

Basic Principles

1. Principle of mutual recognition
2. Principle of pursuit of universal value
3. Principle of basic assistance
4. Principle of mutuality

Items for consideration

1. To liberalize in a selective and phased manner
2. To form national agreement over importation of Japanese popular culture
3. To establish legal and social mechanisms for minimizing the influence of Japanese popular culture
4. To prepare various mechanisms for fostering domestic popular culture mechanisms (The Ministry of Culture and Sports 1994: 196–197)

The emphasis was on liberalization in accordance with the same universal principles that governed commerce with other countries, having accepted that Japanese popular culture had already permeated South Korean society. The report also suggested a specific timeframe: an experiment of phased liberalization from 1995 and total liberalization from 1998, when it anticipated that satellite broadcasting would be regularized.

The report also presents an intriguing perspective on the Otherness of Japanese popular culture.

> Our society has been subjected to the dominant influence of American culture, but we never understand it to be our own. This is because, for us, American culture has a topology as "the Other." As such, when we take in American culture, we can acknowledge each other from a principle of mutuality. However, in the case of Japanese culture, as our social foundation on the receiving end is all too similar to theirs, and there are many things that can be applied without major rearrangement, we easily accept them. Accordingly, our cultural identity is exposed to threat. Only when we recognize Japanese culture as "the Other" can we at last truly comprehend and appraise it. In actuality, for us, Japanese culture is something alien, with extremely strong Otherness, and when appraising Japanese people and Japanese culture, we try to apply the same criteria as to South Koreans and South Korean culture. Although we apply separate standards to a certain extent when assessing other foreign peoples and foreign cultures, as we do not do so in the Japanese case, we experience unnecessary misunderstandings and feelings of betrayal. (The Ministry of Culture and Sports 1994: 198–199)

The report further pointed out that a "stratagem" of "acceptance, starting with things with scant Japanese style" had ultimately generated various contradictions, including numerous practices of plagiarism and imitation, and it advocated exploiting Japanese "Otherness" to minimize the impact of liberalization (The Ministry of Culture and Sports 1994: 198–199). However, the "Otherness" in question here specifically refers to the postcolonial relationship between Japan and South Korea, rather than as a more generalized liberalization strategy. The South Korean public's connection with – and attitude towards – Japanese popular culture had been shaped by the dynamic coexistence of prohibition and trans-bordering for several decades. Thus, in 1994, when the liberalization of Japanese popular culture effectively began, the question posed to South Korean society was not one of choosing between "prohibition or liberalization," but the more fundamental question: "What is Japan, to us?" The dozens of Japan-related books published in 1994 alone are indicative of those epoch-making transformations.

As discussed above, attitudes towards Japanese popular culture changed enormously through the transitions in the media space and cultural consciousness that accompanied globalization, the establishment of an East Asian cultural network, and the reorganization of cultural policy, cultural industries, and the culture-related legal system; and the "prohibitionist" orientation shifted to one of "liberalization." As the geopolitical conditions that had enabled the ban on Japanese popular culture rapidly collapsed, the social fields which had formed the ban – the legal system, the pattern of media practices, and social discourse – were restructured, while at the same time, the "mechanism of negation" in which consciousness and unconsciousness interact in complex ways also transformed from being a "collective consciousness" to being "individual consciousnesses."

However, concerns over the ban itself appear to have been insufficient to progress the processes of "liberalization" on their own. Since the ban on Japanese popular culture was originally a cultural response to having been colonized (decolonization), the process of "liberalization" needed to start with a reexamination of the contradictions inherent to the post-independence decolonization processes. However, despite various reflections and critiques of the violently suppressive military dictatorship and its mechanism of "national mobilization" after democratization, no basic questions were raised about the original impetus for a ban on Japanese style which the new democratic regime had directly inherited, nor about how the military dictatorship had utilized the ban for national mobilization even while maintaining a close relationship with Japan.

This was perhaps because after more than 30 years the ban had become a "taken-for-granted" assumption. Amid continuing conflict between Japan and South Korea over "the historical", anti-Japanese nationalism intensified as hostility towards the Japanese government intertwined with domestic political sentiments, and without any social debate that would cast doubt upon the ban on Japanese popular culture, the only shared "social consciousness" was of its frequent "infringement." Accordingly, the liberalization from the late 1980s merely shifted the discourse seeking to protect "national culture" with a focus on "spiritual domination" and "spiritual resistance" to one prioritizing "cultural industries" comprising "economic domination" and "economic resistance." Ultimately, South Korean society plunged into liberalization and a new age of Japan–South Korea relations without re-examining its ambivalent views and sentiments towards Japanese popular culture.

Hence, the question of how to grasp the historical context of the Japan–South Korea relationship, and how to deal with it, continued to challenge South Korean society. This was in large part because lifting the ban on Japanese popular culture was not a clear or conscious decision by the government, but a series of ad hoc responses as the various contradictions inherent in the prohibition came to light; and because that process further highlighted both the complexities of the post-independence Japan–South Korea relationship, and the nature of Japan-as-the-Other for South Korea.

Chapter 6

CULTURAL EXCHANGE AND THE END OF PROHIBITION

The decades-old ban gave way to the overriding principle of exchange in the new media space. The liberalization of Japanese popular culture was formalized by the state in 1998. At the same time, fresh perspectives and strategies began to be questioned in Japan–South Korea cultural relations.

The liberalization of Japanese popular culture

The Kim Dae-jung government and the liberalization of Japanese popular culture

In October 1998, the government officially announced the liberalization of Japanese popular culture. As discussed in Chapter Five, preparation for that measure had effectively begun on a policy level in 1994. This liberalization was an outcome of the dismantling of the ban on Japanese popular culture, responding to changes in historical and geopolitical conditions since the late 1980s. However, considering the symbolic meaning of the ban in post-independence South Korea, it is clear that the liberalization was not simple. This is evidenced by the fact that previous South Korean governments – such as the Roh Tae-woo and Kim Young-sam administrations, which had touted opening-up and globalization, pitching an extremely forward-looking stance vis-à-vis the liberalization of Japanese popular culture both within and outside the country – ultimately had not dismantled the ban. Kumamoto Shin'ichi, a reporter for the *Asahi Shinbun* who had covered the Japan–South Korea cultural relationship for many years, wrote: "And yet, looking back on the history of Japan–South Korea relations, I think that the liberalization policy this time is a 'bold decision,' and its ripple effect will also be large" (*The Asahi Shinbun* 1998b).

The formation of the Kim Dae-jung administration in 1998 was seen as a departure from the 1965 system of Japan–South Korea relations, largely because it was free from both the political liabilities of a martial regime and the perception of being pro-Japanese. These issues were outlined by the then-presidential candidate Kim Dae-jung during the 1997 presidential election campaign, which had been dubbed a "showdown" between Park Chung-hee and Kim Dae-jung.

> Former President Park Chung-hee was also a typical member of the pro-Japanese faction [colonial collaborators]. After Liberation, the pro-Japanese faction treated democratic forces that had campaigned for independence as pro-communist and quashed them; and following the April 19 Revolution, it transformed into an anti-democratic force for the military. If we assume former President Syngman Rhee to have pretended to be pro-Japanese, then we could call former President Park a genuine pro-Japanese influence. (*The Kyunghyang Shinmun* 1997)

The fact that President Kim was not tainted by perceptions of belonging to the pro-Japanese faction was arguably crucial in facilitating his promotion of liberalizing Japanese popular culture. As former Culture Minister Lee O-young stated, for the South Korean government, suspicions of being pro-Japanese had been a huge burden in promoting such liberalization.

> Major newspapers that argue it is too soon for liberalization of Japanese popular culture are a big stumbling-block. As I am seen as pro-Japanese [*in that I am well-versed in Japanese affairs*], this makes it even more difficult. (*The Asahi Shinbun* 1998b, emphasis added)

Kim Dae-jung's personal attitude and the Kim administration's policy towards Japan makes clear that South Korean society's perceptions of Japan cannot be reduced to a simplistic schema that equates criticism of the pro-Japanese faction with "anti-Japanese" sentiments. As observed earlier in this book, the conflicting perceptions and attitudes regarding the pro-Japanese faction are direct products of the historical formation and transition of authority in the South Korean domestic context; and, as the attitudes of each administration to Japanese popular culture show, it cannot be understood solely through the frame of Japan–South Korea relations. In other words, it is quite possible to be both critical of the pro-Japanese faction and welcoming of stronger connections with Japan. In fact, Kim Dae-jung readily acknowledged that he was "well-versed in Japanese affairs", as the Japanese news media never failed to mention following his election.

In liberalizing Japanese popular culture, President Kim reportedly instructed the relevant departments to "Tackle it without fear" (*The Dong-A Ilbo* 1998). This marks a significant turnaround, from a political order that had for several decades governed in fear of Japanese culture to one ordered to "not fear" it. Ultimately, the greatest significance of the 1998 liberalization of Japanese popular culture by the Kim Dae-jung administration was probably its impact on perceptions and attitudes towards Japan-the-Other.

The Asian currency crisis and economic opening to Japan

The ban on Japanese popular culture, which hitherto had been understood primarily from a political perspective, began to be discussed as an important economic issue from the late 1990s. The forces of globalization lay in the background, but the decisive precursor was the 1997 Asian currency crisis.

Since the 1965 normalization of diplomatic relations between Japan and the Republic of Korea, economic connections between the two countries had expanded and strengthened even while maintaining South Korea's ambivalent attitude towards Japanese popular culture. While heavily reliant on imported industrial products, products that were made in Japan were still restricted on the grounds of a trade deficit and national sentiment. In this context, the Asian currency crisis in the midst of rapidly advancing globalization had a huge impact on the economic relationships between Japan and South Korea, also.

The biggest change was the abolition of South Korea's import source diversification system, which had controlled the market access of Japanese products. From June 1999, bans were lifted on the importation of sixteen items by Japanese manufacturers, including motor vehicles, large-scale televisions, and mobile telephones, marking the total abolition of restrictions on imports from Japan after twenty-one years. The import source diversification system had originally been introduced in 1978 with the aim of addressing the trade imbalance with Japan. In its peak period in the early 1980s, the importation of 924 items, mainly electronic or electrical devices, motor vehicles and machinery, was restricted, but in negotiations with the World Trade Organization (WTO) in 1996 South Korea agreed to its phased reduction by the end of 1999; and, as a condition for receiving financial assistance from the International Monetary Fund (IMF) following the 1997 Asian financial crisis, totally abolished the sixteen remaining items half a year sooner than scheduled.

The liberalization of Japanese popular culture was entwined with this trend of opening market access to Japanese goods. Many reports on economic or cultural issues reiterated the need for the liberalization of Japanese popular culture, and various strategies were proposed for turning the entry of Japanese goods and popular culture into an opportunity to bolster the competitiveness of Korean goods and popular culture, and to build a new relationship between Japan and South Korea.

For example, the following column was carried in the April 1999 edition of the monthly advertising bulletin published by KOBACO (Korean Broadcast Advertising Corporation) which operates and controls South Korean broadcast advertising.

Japanese products and Japanese culture which have been barred in various ways for the half-century or so since Liberation will be coming to South Korea. For these fifty years, Koreans have experienced all kinds of emotional fluctuations, from extreme anti-Japanese feeling to a yearning for good-quality Japanese goods, and ultimately to young people's positive response to Japanese culture… The influx of Japanese goods, culture and advertising has become a challenge in the South Korean advertising world. Japan has been a model for the expansion of Korean industry, and the advertising community, too, has been no exception… If Japanese popular culture and the importation of goods are liberalized, then self-censorship towards plagiarism will probably need to be tightened. Brazen purloining is likely to lessen, and, by the deepening of advertisers' understanding of the differences between Japanese and Korean consumers' mentality and culture, advertising is likely to create opportunities to fill the gulf that has existed for fifty years between the feelings of Japan and South Korea. (Song 1999: 40–41)

The national catastrophe of the Asian financial crisis, in particular, became a decisive turning-point when the culture industry became a significant sector in the South Korean economy. Amid the perception that the developmental state period marked the beginning of the economic crisis, attempts to reposition popular culture – which had hitherto been seen as merely peripheral to industrialization – as a key driver of national competitiveness came to be seen as a crucial undertaking. This change in focus is evident in expressions such as "cultural policy for a second nation-building," "twenty-first-century culture enters the country," and "a nation with top-ranking culture" in reports published by the Ministry of Culture and Tourism of South Korea. Promotion of the culture industry was thus positioned as one of the main axes of state policy from the beginning of the Kim Dae-jung regime (The Ministry of Culture and Tourism of South Korea 2000). In 1999 the "Basic Law on Cultural Industry Promotion" was enacted, and from 2000 the Culture Industry Promotion Foundation established with financial support of a hundred billion won (The Ministry of Culture and Tourism of South Korea 2000).

In short, the liberalization of Japanese popular culture was unavoidable in the so-called "IMF age" from 1997 onwards. It was not simply a response to conditions attached to economic aid from Japan, but occurred against the backdrop of a national decision to grow the cultural industry and compete in the world market. Thus, amid a complex mix of anxiety and expectation, fear and hope, Japanese popular culture transformed from an issue of cultural politics to one of cultural economics.

Co-hosting the World Cup and the Japan–South Korea "2002 system"

In the midst of these rapidly changing political and economic conditions, cultural relations between the two nations were also radically transformed. Undoubtedly, the sign of this was their co-hosting of the soccer World Cup.

On October 21, 1998, the South Korean government explained the significance of the first-phase liberalization, which targeted films, manga, and magazines, using terms such as "establishment of policy with national agreement," a "phased and positive approach," "mutuality," "wholesome cultural exchange," and "promotion of commercial exchange."

> At this point in time, when lively cultural exchange between South Korea and Japan is starting up on the momentum of the joint hosting of the 2002 World Cup, the life of the so-called "1965 system" has begun to end, and the "2002 system" is already about to arise anew. Moreover, the world is entering an age of unlimited competition where all things are being liberalized for each other's mutual prosperity as a borderless global village. Amid such an international trend, it is unnatural not to conduct cultural exchange with a specific state. (The Ministry of Culture and Tourism of South Korea 1998, emphasis added)

Japanese Prime Minister Obuchi Keizō and South Korean President Kim Dae-jung announced the Japan–South Korea Joint Declaration, stating: "With the acknowledgement that there is deep mutual understanding and diverse exchange between the people of our two nations that is not limited to government-to-government exchange, we shall henceforth expand cultural and personal exchange between our two nations." The liberalization of Japanese popular culture was central to the Japan–South Korea Joint Declaration of a "new Japan–South Korea Partnership aimed at the twenty-first century."

> President Kim Dae-jung conveyed his policy of opening-up to Japanese culture in South Korea, and Prime Minister Obuchi welcomed this policy as being something that would lead to true mutual understanding between Japan and South Korea. Along with declaring a shared conviction that the "new Japan–South Korea Partnership aimed at the Twenty-first Century" could be expanded into something of an even higher dimension by broad participation and unremitting effort on the part of the people of both nations, Prime Minister Obuchi and President Kim Dae-jung called upon the people of both nations to share the spirit of this Joint Declaration, and participate in a shared task aimed at the establishment and growth of a new Japan–South Korea partnership. (The Ministry of Foreign Affairs of Japan 1998)

According to Chi Myung-Kwan, Director of Hallym University's Institute of Japanese Studies and the inaugural Chair of South Korea's South Korea–Japan Cultural Exchange Policy Advisory Committee, this "2002 system" signified:

> a new system in which [we] jointly hosted the World Cup, and the people of both South Korea and Japan made an amicable settlement, [moving on] from the 1965 system, which had been confined to rehabilitation of a political and economic relationship through the South Korea–Japan treaty [for normalization of relations]. (*The Asahi Shinbun* 1998a)

In other words, departure from the 1965 system, which had defined postwar Japan–South Korea relations for decades, had become a combined Japan–South Korea objective. To some extent, this new relationship between Japan and South Korea was shaped by the rising self-consciousness of "East Asia" which had begun to emerge in the 1990s. Political and economic relations that had been defined by the Cold War structure and the processes of industrialization had begun to fall apart across the region, and new ways of conceiving East Asia had begun. Culture, symbolized by the liberalization of Japanese popular culture, was central to these new conceptions, and the question of how cultural exchange could serve to establish new Japan–South Korea relations independently of politics and economics became the central issue of the 2002 system.

A new generation rejects negation

As discussed above, the liberalization of Japanese popular culture was a political, economic and cultural transformation generated by numerous changes in historical conditions. To fully apprehend its character, it is necessary to understand the substantive change in the cultural sensitivity of the receivers of Japanese popular culture, which extended far beyond the realms of cultural policy and cultural industries. These changes occurred as postmodernism entered the South Korean cultural space from the 1990s, and the grand narrative that had hitherto dominated South Korean society was dismantled. With the end of the Cold War, democratization, and opening-up, individuals' desires and values emerged as the primary cultural factor. Popular culture, which had been treated as both inferior and threatening by national governments since independence, was repositioned as a core social field, and as the production, distribution and consumption of new subcultures became ever more popular, consumers of Japanese popular culture ceased to be seen as "national citizens", but were regarded instead as atomistic individuals. A 1995 poem titled "Love of Seun Sangga KIDS" by the poet Yoo Ha, who entered the limelight in 1988 when South Korea was riding the currents of a new age, and was a leading figure of literary postmodernism in South Korea throughout the 1990s, succinctly expressed these changes.

> I learned English
> From pirated American novels
> And the *Reader's Digest*,
> And loved to sing only banned songs
> Vanished even from pirated records
> The smell of Building 3 that was my territory, and "Blue Light Yokohama"

Punks, holes in the school walls
and the live-house bands of Seun Sangga
I loved every kind of transgression
And loved nothing but discarded curses and slang
(Yoo 1995: 104–105)

This poem sings of the cultural sensitivity of South Korean society in which prohibition and infringement intermixed in complex ways. The Seun Sangga mentioned here was an electronics shopping complex completed in 1967 in Seoul's Jongno Ward which symbolized South Korea's modernization during the developmental dictatorship period. Behind this huge building, called a "dream of modernization," we can imagine the narrator encountered all kinds of things that would be "prohibited" in front of it.

Yoo Ha's poem was characterized as post-modern arguably because of its rejection of the grand narrative which dominated the national order until then, and its emphasis on individual desire. Post-modernism in South Korea was characterized by the recon-ceptualization of "the subject" from "nationals" to "individuals," as seen in the wildly enthusiastic reaction to works by Japanese author Murakami Haruki including his *Norwegian Wood*, which presented an individual perspective and individual experience. South Koreans as "nationals" had been expected to refuse the consumption of Japanese popular culture, but Yoo Ha's poem explicitly rejects this expectation, recounting experiences based on individual desires and the individual's love of those desires.

Of course, this change in consciousness was not only, or even primarily, in response to Japan. Rather, it was because the basis for the ban which until then had been central to the grand narrative disappeared as South Korean attitudes towards popular culture changed, and the importance of individual agency came to the fore; the refusal to reject became commonplace amid the growing emphasis on encounters based on individual ideas and desires, undermining the ban on Japanese popular culture.

The generation born in the 1970s, who had been socialized with the patterns of capitalist consumption through video culture and color television since early childhood, were early adopters of new media such as computers and pagers, and sought to discover the world from a private space centered upon themselves. Their enthusiasm for rap music, which set individual feelings towards society – not society itself – to rhythm, and for consumer spaces where desire alone – not personal obligation – was prioritized, can be seen as cultural expressions of individual desires. The subjects of this new consumer culture were of a generation that was comparatively free from any sense of inferiority vis-à-vis U.S. or Japanese popular culture, most evident in their attitudes to Japanese popular culture. Thus a huge gap opened between the generations, which further undermined the ban which had been accommodated by the older (Japanese-language and industrialized) generations.

In the 1990s, the younger generation rejected criticism of its cultural activities and sought to reposition the consumption of Japanese popular culture as a sort of public culture, rather than private deviant behavior. A new kind of fandom formed, centered on prominent Japanese artists, such as X JAPAN and Miyazaki Hayao, Murakami Haruki, *SLAM DUNK*, *Neon Genesis Evangelion* etc. Universities experienced an increase in the numbers of study groups, clubs for screening Japanese films, anime, and musical appreciation salons. The pirated version of X JAPAN's album, "BLUE BLOOD" reportedly sold more than 500,000 copies (*Cine 21* 2009).

> One day in April 1996, when an "Exhibition of contemporary works from 1980s~90s Japanese film festivals" held in the main auditorium at Yonsei University had entered its middle phase, ... that spacious auditorium was packed with spectators who had descended upon it... That day's screening of *Love Letter* caused a ripple, and its wavelength expanded inexorably. The question "*O-genki desu ka?* (Are you well?)" became the first step to learning Japanese, ... and [the pop singer and actress] Nakayama Miho who played [the dual roles of] Watanabe Hiroko and Fujii Itsuki was identified with the purity of first love. And 300,000 videotapes reproduced without permission went all around the country; and finally, young people numbering one million ended up accepting *Love Letter*, which had wafted in from a young director called Iwai Shunji from the Japanese Archipelago, as their own story. (*Kino* 1999)

155

In short, the Japan boom of the 1990s was completely different to previous waves of consumption of Japanese popular culture. Whereas universities until the 1980s had been the site of countless campaigns protesting the dictatorships and U.S. hegemony, in the 1990s they screened Japanese films and anime and hosted rock concerts, expressing much more than a simple change of era. For young people of the 1990s, who had grown up with depoliticization, personalization, and global perspective that incorporated East Asia, perceptions and attitudes towards Japan the Other were totally divorced from those of the older generation. As the South Korean cultural space was radically transformed, Japanese popular culture became one of the cornerstones of the postmodern cultural space.

University students' attitudes towards Japanese popular culture were strikingly expressed in surveys from 1998 when the liberalization of Japanese popular culture was formally announced. According to a survey of university students in the Seoul area, conducted by the South Korean *Daehak Sinmun* (University Newspaper), 84.2 percent of respondents replied that Japanese popular culture had exerted a "Large: influence on South Korean society; and 90.0 percent replied that they had come into contact with Japanese anime and manga,

Image 6.1:
The cover of the December 1998 issue of *Kino* promotes Japanese films after the liberalization of Japanese popular culture was formally announced

popular music, television, magazines etc. Moreover, 84.1 percent expressed support for the government's phased liberalization policy (*Daehak Shinmun* 1998). Hence, where "national sentiment" and the "protection of youth" had been the justification for banning Japanese popular culture, those grounds did not apply to the youth culture of the 1990s.

The monthly cinema magazine, *Kino*, launched in 1995, was widely read by university students and culture enthusiasts. It provides a clear example of the changes in South Korean perceptions and attitudes towards Japanese popular culture in the 1990s. From its first issue, *Kino* profiled Japanese films and anime, providing the latest news from its Tokyo correspondent, along with deep analyses of both new and older works. A very high proportion of each issue was devoted to Japanese works, including a special feature on Japanese cinema based on an interview with the chief editor of the Japanese film magazine, *Kinema Junpō*, in the December 1995 issue, and consecutive special features on Japanese anime in the November and December 1996 issues. While Hollywood movies and European art films had previously been an important focus of the discourse on cinema, Japanese films and anime largely displaced them in the 1990s.

This iteration of Japanese films and anime was situated within a new frame of "Asian cinema." Alongside Japanese films and South Korean cinema, Asian directors in the international limelight, including Hong Kong's John Woo, China's Chen Kaige, Taiwan's Ang Lee and Hou Hsiao-Hsien, and Vietnam's Trần Anh Hùng were defining Asian cinema, which was on the cusp of a new period of prosperity. The cultural dynamism generated by East Asia's opening transformed the consumption mechanisms that had developed around the ban on Japanese popular culture, which, in turn, transformed the media space. The new openness to Japanese culture was clearly evident when, in 1998, Kurosawa Akira died, and *Kino* published a special feature in commemoration.

Most of the film directors who could trigger creation seem to have left this world. Here, we must farewell Mr. Akira Kurosawa with feelings of heartbreak. Giants have left our side, and we that remain on Earth steadily grow less significant. Just as literature has lost Dostoevsky, and nobody can make up for that sense of loss, so can the place vacated by Kurosawa never again be filled by anyone. However, just like Sanjūrō who swaggers off and glances back, Kurosawa would surely say to us as we lament: 'Idiots! From here on, it is your time, so from now on you are adults.' That's right, Maestro. Sayonara, Kurosawa. (*Kino* 1998)

This passage, written the year that Japanese popular culture was officially liberated, reveals how much Japanese culture had already been absorbed by South Korean audiences. In the 1990s media space, a new generation had started to take the lead in shaping the cultural landscape with a more fluid and, indeed, global sensitivity that transcended concerns about cultural trans-bordering from Japan or the U.S. garrisons. This new cultural frame was shared by a new generation of individualist consumers who openly embraced Japanese popular culture.

On the premise that the legal system's vague approach to copyright issues became problematic for media practices, and that opening-up and democratization forced changes in the "mechanisms of prohibition," it follows that changes in collective attitudes towards Japanese popular culture raised questions about the prohibition in social discourse. Assuming that improvements to the legal system and reorganization of the industrial system made overt enforcement of the ban impossible, then the changing attitudes of individual subjects who embraced the consumption of Japanese popular culture rendered the pursuit of prohibition by self-censorship pointless.

The collision of culture and history

The implementation of phased liberalization

In the context of such significant shifts in the political, economic and cultural fields, the ban on Japanese popular culture was dismantled through a phased liberalization. Let us summarize this process from the first-stage liberalization in 1998 until the fourth-stage liberalization in 2004.

Table 6.1: Four stages of liberalization

Date of liberalization	Content to be liberalized
First stage October 20, 1998	1) Film and video • Works awarded prizes at [any of the] four major international film festivals (Cannes, Venice, Berlin, Academy Awards), and Japanese-Korean joint film productions • Permission for Japanese actors to perform in Korean films, and for Japanese-Korean film festivals • "Video" refers to videos of Japanese films screened in Korea after the announcement of liberalization 2) Publications • Japanese-language versions of manga, and manga magazines
Second stage September 10, 1999	1) Expansion of liberalization of film and video category • Works awarded prizes at officially recognized international film festivals • Films that our nation's Film Classification Committee has designated as "For General Exhibition" (excluding cinema-version animation) 2) Live performances • Performance of Japanese popular songs in indoor venues with 2000 seats or fewer (However, the broadcasting of performances at food and hospitality venues, and the production and sale of sound or video recordings of live performances are not permitted)
Third stage June 27, 2000	Film • Additional liberalization to encompass films recognized by the Film Classification Committee as "Viewing permissible for 12 years and up" and "Viewing permissible for 15-years and up" * No liberalization for films "Viewing not permissible for under 18s" 2) Cinema-version animation • Works awarded prizes at all types of international film festivals, including international animated film festivals 3) Video • Videos of films and animated films screened domestically 4) Public performance of popular songs • Total opening-up, regardless of whether indoors or outdoors 5) Music disks • All music disks, except sound disks of Japanese-language songs (musical performance, singing in languages from neither Korea nor Japan, translations into Korean language, etc.) 6) Games • All games (PC games, online games, games for amusement-center use, etc.), but excluding video games 7) Broadcasting • Broadcast of sports, documentaries and news programs, without classification of medium • In the case of cable television and satellite broadcasting, works awarded prizes at officially recognized international film festivals, and domestically-released films permitted for general exhibition
Fourth stage January 1, 2004	1) Films: total liberalization 2) Recorded disks: total liberalization, including Japanese-language music disks 3) Games: total liberalization 4) Video: expanded the breadth of liberalization in partnership with film and cinema-version animation 5) Broadcasting: broad liberalization of cable television and satellite broadcasting, and partial liberalization of terrestrial broadcast signals * Target of restriction • Popular songs: terrestrial telecasts of music videos with Japanese-language songs • Television dramas: liberalization restricted to jointly-produced Japanese–Korean dramas in the case of terrestrial broadcast signals • All variety programs 6) Cinema-version animation • Complete liberalization from January 1, 2006

One point to note is a delay between the third- (2000) and fourth-stage liberalization (2004). Why was the process interrupted in 2001, although liberalization had proceeded every year since its first stage in 1998? Behind this, new historical issues surfaced.

The 2001 Textbook Issue

One year before the 2002 World Cup, in an atmosphere of unprecedented cordiality towards Japan (described as the "best in history") (*The Mainichi Shinbun* 2001), the sudden deterioration of the relationship between Japan and South Korea was triggered by the publication of middle-school history textbooks edited by the Japanese Group to make new history textbooks (*Atarashī rekishi kyōkasho wo tsukuru kai*) and authorized by the Japanese Ministry of Education, Culture, Sports, Science and Technology in April 2001. This publication by Fusosha provoked a backlash from both within and outside Japan.

Particularly problematic in South Korea were the descriptions of the colonial period, especially about the "Donghak rebellion," "forced annexation of Korea," "military comfort women," and the "imperialization policy." For example, Fusosha's *New History Textbooks* referred to the "Donghak rebellion" – an event memorialized in South Korea as a campaign to defend the country from invading foreigners – as the "Donghak peasant uprising" – or, a mere peasant uprising; and although the book mentioned the forced participation of the so-called "comfort women," it did not describe the great harm done to women and children across Asia, nor did it employ the term *jūgun ianfu* (military comfort women) (Kano & Tsuchiya 2002: 25–30).

This was embarrassing for the Kim Dae-jung administration, which had pushed through the Japan–South Korea Joint Declaration and the liberalization of Japanese popular culture despite strong domestic opposition. The rekindling of this issue of "historical recognition" put a dampener on Kim's "sunshine policy" towards Japan. Under pressure from the conservative newspapers, and faced with a resolution in the National Assembly "to urge the rectification of distortions in Japanese national history textbooks," in July 2001 the government cancelled all liberalization measures scheduled for the end of 2001 and 2002, explaining that "as the liberalization of Japanese popular culture [wa]s something implemented upon the basis of a relationship of mutual trust between the two nations of South Korea and Japan, the additional liberalization of Japanese popular culture cannot be separated from the problem of distortion in Japanese history textbooks" (*Yonhap News* 2001).

This textbook issue not only heightened anxiety and concerns that Japan was becoming increasingly right-wing, it also weakened efforts within South Korea to critically re-examine South Korean nationalism. Efforts to break the framework of the nation-state and counter the political-right through the critical civil society were also bound to be dampened.

This conflict created a dilemma in South Korean society. Not only did the government suspend the next phase of liberalization, but it also created problems for many cultural exchange events that had been scheduled. In short, for the South Korean government and re-lated bodies – which had sincerely embraced the need for improved cultural exchange between Japan and South Korea – the circumstances made it "possible neither to continue nor to suspend" these events (*The Dong-A Ilbo* 2001).

Eventually, the fourth stage of liberalization was recommenced in 2004 by the Roh Moo-hyun administration, inaugurated in 2003. This was ultimately a result of the cordial relations developed through co-hosting the 2002 World Cup, despite the backlash against the text-book issue.

Nevertheless, the dilemma produced by this textbook issue signifi-cantly shaped the character of the 2002 system. The conflict forced Japan and South Korea to recognize that they were not yet rid of the 1965 system, in spite of the brisk cultural exchanges of the 2000s. In short, the unprecedented cultural exchange between Japan and South Korea unfolded in circumstances in which there were always sparks of enmity.

The market for Japanese popular culture contracts

The pause in phased liberalization between 2001 and 2003 had a significant impact on the market for Japanese popular culture in South Korea. This appeared most markedly in the film industry which had been officially opening since 1998. Iwai Shunji's *Love Letter*, released in November 1999, was the most popular film in South Korea, mobilizing an audience of 640,000 in Seoul (1.2 million nationwide). According to *Kino* magazine's January 2000 issue, *Love Letter* was number one in "Readers' choice of best ten films of 1999–2000" and director Imamura Shinji's Shōhei's *Unagi* (The Eel) and *Narayamabushikō* (The Ballad of Narayama) took seventh and eighth place. Despite terrestrial television advertisements for *Love Letter* having been prohibited by an obscure decision of the Broadcasting Committee, which stated: "[As] Japanese culture has not been completely liberalized, advertising using a medium with major ramifications such as terrestrial television broadcasting will be possible *after* Japanese culture has been wholly liberalized" (*Yonhap News* 1999, emphasis added), cinema fans in South Korea went wild over this story, with people who had already watched it on pirated videotapes heading to cinemas multiple times.

> Iwai Shunji's *Love Letter*, which had been drifting around like a ghost for these three years through gatherings to screen illegal videos and illegally copied videotapes, was formally introduced in concert with the second-stage liberalization of Japanese films. The film's success has "exceeded expectations", and all of the cinema seats for the remainder of 1999 have already sold out, it being on

Image 6.2:
A newspaper advertisement for the opening of *Love Letter*
(*The Kyunghyang Shinmun* 1999)

the date agenda for staying up all night at the end of the century...
Is this strange phenomenon of watching it again and again [due
to] the power of *Love Letter*, or the power of Japanese cinema?
(*Kino* 2000)

Japanese films' share of the South Korean cinema market jumped from
3.1 percent in 1999 (based on Seoul movie theaters) to 7.4 percent in 2000.
In 2000, nine films each mobilized more than 100,000 people in Seoul:
Odoru daisōsasen (Bayside Shakedown) (309,767), *Shall We Dance?*
(301,692), *SF samurai fikushon* (Samurai Fiction) (224,256), *Poppoya*
(Railroad Man) (219,327 attendees), *Gekijōban poketto monsutā Myūtsū
no gyakushū* (Pokémon the Movie: Mewtwo Strikes Back) (182,360),
Shigatsu monogatari (April Story) (161,423), *Ai no korīda* (In the Realm
of the Senses) (141,115), *Rajio no jikan* (Welcome Back, Mr. McDonald)
(137,063), *Ringu 2* (Ring 2) (128,521) (Film Promotion Committee 2000;
Korea Culture and Tourism Policy Institute 2003).

However, the Japanese film market share nose-dived to 1.4 percent
in 2001, rebounding slightly to 3.2 percent in 2002. Two of the four
films that mobilized audiences of more than 100,000 in 2001 and
2002 in Seoul were director Miyazaki Hayao's *Tonari no Totoro* (My
Neighbor Totoro) (released in 2001; 128,900 attendees in Seoul) and
Sen to Chihiro no Kamikakushi (Spirited Away) (released 2002; 936,250
attendees in Seoul). The rapid increase in South Korean films' market
share from 35.8 percent in 1999 and 32.0 percent in 2000 to 46.1 percent
in 2001 and 45.2 percent in 2002 may partially explain the collapse in
Japanese market-share; but considering the vibrance of the Japanese
film market in 2000, this phenomenon could not be fully explained by
that factor alone.

Until the second half of 2000, after the third stage of liberalization,
the box office for Japanese films maintained its balance. *Odoru
daisōsasen* (Bayside Shakedown), boasting the underlying strength
of the Japanese blockbuster, attracted an audience of 610,000
(hereafter, figures on a nationwide basis, cited by the author), and
Gekijōban Poketto Monsutā Myūtsū no Gyakushū (Pokémon the
Movie: Mewtwo Strikes Back) attracted an audience of 600,000,
the most for a Japanese anime. It was after this that the box office

for Japanese films quietened. Was that a coincidence? It was at this time that the "problem of distortion in history textbooks" emerged as a social issue. One person involved stated: "I do not have precise data, but it is hard to say that the slump in the box office for Japanese films is unrelated to anti-Japanese sentiment." (*Maekyung City Life* 2001)

The sudden change in attitudes towards Japanese popular culture after the emergence of the textbook issue erupted is also apparent in a dispute over the airing on February 15–16, 2002 of the television drama, *Friends*, a Japanese–South Korean joint production by TBS and MBC (no relation to the long-running American sitcom of the same name). The trigger for this dispute was that approximately 30 percent of the dialogue was in Japanese. Chi Myung-Kwan, then Chair of the South Korea–Japan Cultural Exchange Policy Advisory Committee resigned, stating: "I protest the unprincipled acceptance of Japanese culture by our country's government and broadcasters." Chi went on to criticize the Ministry of Culture and Tourism and the Broadcasting Committee for having "neglectfully allowed the airing of a drama containing Japanese language on terrestrial television, which has not been officially liberalized." Chi also deplored the actions of MBC, saying: "Despite the fact that a subtle current of air has been flowing around the Japan–South Korea relationship because of repercussions from the distortions in Japanese history textbooks, [MBC] has ignored public decisions due to its commercialism, and has turned its back upon the public good" (*The Dong-A Ilbo* 2002a). *Dong-A Ilbo*, in turn, published a critique of the incident in its editorial the following day:

> This drama was telecast over two days, but during that time there were no sanctions whatsoever. This means that both the Ministry of Culture and Broadcasting Committee had let it go... The World Cup and the liberalization of Japanese popular culture are separate issues. Even by deliberation after the fact, the relevant authorities should reprimand those involved from the broadcasting station, and challenge them to thorough checks to ensure observance of the principles of phased liberalization of Japanese popular culture. (*The Dong-A Ilbo* 2002b)

In response, MBC pointed out that "the airing of programs in the form of South Korean–Japanese joint productions should be decided upon in consideration of national interest, public opinion and culture" (*The Hankook Ilbo* 2002), and challenged the suggestion that it should exercise "restraint simply for the reason that there is Japanese dialogue" (*The Dong-A Ilbo* 2002a), noting that "their telecast is possible because those dramas have also received an authoritative interpretation from the Broadcasting Committee, saying that they are South Korean–Japanese co-productions, not *Japanese* dramas" (*The Hankook Ilbo* 2002, emphasis added). The Broadcasting Committee's response that "programs which are South Korean–Japanese joint productions are not the target of the Japanese culture liberalization policy" indicates that there were no established standards relating to co-produced programs. Against the background of the South Korean government permitting the broadcast of songs in Japanese from February to July 2002, and the numerous cultural exchanges associated with the World Cup, these criticisms of the liberalization of Japanese popular culture can be seen as an extension of the textbook issue.

The textbook issue struck a blow to the market for Japanese popular culture, and impacted the social discourses of Japan–South Korea cultural exchange. Naturally, conflicts in the Japan–South Korea relationship were nothing new. However, considering that primary consumers of culture in the age of the so-called "2002 system" were comparatively free from the mechanisms of prohibition of the "1965 system," we could not reduce their perceptions and feelings over Japanese popular culture to the "anti-Japanese sentiment" of the past.

The difference is clear also from a survey entitled "Liberalization relating to Japanese broadcasting" carried out by the Broadcasting Committee in August 2002, immediately after the World Cup. In response to the question: "Should the progressive liberalization of Japanese broadcasting be linked with the distortions in Japanese history textbooks?" 61.6 percent of respondents answered "no" (*OhmyNews* 2002). In short, this historical issue arguably raised a mixture of complex and ambiguous feelings among the new consumer stratum in South Korea who had not been subjected to the "mechanisms of negation" of the 1965 system.

From 1998, the consumption of Japanese popular culture in South Korea did not court social criticism due to conscience, as it had previously. Instead, a different form of negation arose with antipathy towards Japan's treatment of history. If we assume that Japanese popular culture in the 1965 system was consumed in ways that did not overtly express positive feelings about that culture, its consumption in the 2000s transformed into a form which, while not hiding feelings or personal tastes, simultaneously expressed a publicly shared political obligation.

A new approach to Japan–South Korea cultural relations

The impact of the Korean wave

As discussed above, the liberalization of Japanese popular culture happened in the context of globalization, opening-up, and complex changes in the political, economic and cultural relationship with Japan. However, another factor that dramatically changed perceptions of cultural industries in unexpected ways was known as the "Korean wave" (Chinese: *Hanliu*; Korean: *Hallyu*; Japanese: *Kanryū*) which began in China in the late 1990s.

South Korean television dramas had become increasingly popular in China since 1997. After *Beijing Qingnian Bao* (Beijing Youth Daily) described the popularity of South Korean singing idols as "*Hanliu*" in 1999, the inflow of South Korean popular culture began to be referred to as a "Korean wave."

> The west wind may also come from the east. Nowadays, when eastern culture and western culture are both in vogue, everything that can be popular seems to turn into a boom. Now, the flock of "Korean wave" enthusiasts who were crazy about [the South Korean singing duo] Clon, clad in metal armor, have hands full of information flyers for [the boy band] H.O.T. (*Beijing Qingnian Bao*, 19 November 1999, as cited in the Ministry of Culture, Sports, and Tourism of South Korea 2013: 16)

With rapidly growing export revenues from television programs ($12.74 million in 1999; $14 million in 2000), the Korean wave was reported in the South Korean news media from 2000, and by 2001 was a widely recognized phenomenon. Entertainment production agencies in South Korea, led by H.O.T's agency, SM Entertainment, began to capitalize on the Korean wave in China and South-East Asia, and the South Korean government incorporated it into its cultural policy.

For South Korean society, which had long focused on protecting the domestic industry from American and Japanese trans-bordering, the Korean wave fundamentally changed perceptions that had endured for decades. In that context, the changes in perception and the strategic plan for popular culture that developed in response to the Korean wave prompted a change in strategy vis-à-vis Japanese popular culture.

> The Korean wave storm has not simply stopped at giving the young people of China good feelings about our country's culture, but has also directly and indirectly contributed to the advance of our country's goods into China... It is an example that has plainly indicated the potential for our culture to sell in foreign markets, as well... However, our country will not be able to become a powerful nation in the entertainment [realm] just by means of a short-term promotion policy from the government. Nor will it be able to enhance the competitiveness of domestic industry by a conservative policy that prevents the importation of foreign cultural products. It has become impossible to maintain the existing taboo perceived to exist in relation to the importation of Japanese cultural commodities any further. Ultimately, the only way will be for us ourselves to raise our competitiveness, with the combined efforts of the government and the private sector. (*Maeil Business Newspaper* 2001a)

In academia, the Korean wave became an important theme for under-standing the East Asian media space. The permeation of Japanese popular culture through the East Asian region in the 1990s had been the central focus of research into the East Asian cultural order (Iwabuchi 2002; Shiraishi 2007). This new Korean wave now situated South Korea – hitherto merely a peripheral consumer of Japanese popular culture –

as a leading culture-producing nation, which significantly changed the direction of research on the East Asian cultural order. In the initial stage of Korean wave studies in South Korea in 2003, cultural anthropologist Chohan He-jeong described it as a "global indication of a seismic shift."

> The *Hallyu* (Korean wave) boom is something that has spread since the late 1990s among the residents of China, followed by Taiwan, Hong Kong, Vietnam and so forth, especially among young people, and that indicates a tendency to enjoy and consume South Korean popular culture such as songs, [television] dramas, fashion, tourism, films and the like. This is an event that has arisen in linkage with a multilayered migration phenomenon, including the migration of transnational capital, and is a deeply meaningful development expressing a strong desire by the residents of East Asia who have come to obtain some degree of economic power through a compressed process of modernization to become the subjects of their perceptions by enjoying the popular culture not of the West, but of East Asia. (Chohan 2003: 3)

In many respects, this passage is almost identical to descriptions of Japanese popular culture in the 1990s. However, the Korean wave was markedly different to the spread of Japanese popular culture. These new markets had much more in common with South Korea, as a peripheral country that had experienced rapid industrialization in the late twentieth century, than with Japan, which had industrialized decades earlier and played the role of a "core state" in the Asian region throughout the Cold War era.

These developments deeply affected the self-awareness of South Korean society, producing a diverse "*Hallyu* discourse" incorporating cultural nationalism, postcolonialism, neoliberalism, among other things. Of course, it also generated a critical counter-discourse (by a comparative minority), which characterized the *Hallyu* discourse as "a patriotism based on an [inferiority] complex of the residents of surrounding countries" (Chohan 2003: 13–15) and a "childish cultural supremacy" (Lee 2005: 203), which could also be called a South Korean version of Japanese "soft nationalism" (Iwabuchi 2002) which focused on the worldwide diffusion of Japanese-made media, software and content in terms of national interest. This marked the real beginning of conflict over the meaning of the lively consumption in Asian countries of South Korean popular culture, which had taken shape while mainly responding to and imitating "American-like" and "Japanese-like" cultural products. The discovery of South Korean culture by the East Asian market also had a huge impact on perceptions and attitudes towards Japanese popular culture.

Perceptions and strategies around Japan–South Korea cultural exchange

In a 2002 report, Samsung Economic Research Institute classified the issues relating to the liberalization of the cultural market into seven categories: cultural identity; breadth of liberalization; capital inflow; content inflow; operator inflow; post-liberalization cultural policy; and post-liberalization overseas expansion. The Korean wave subsequently ushered in new perceptions and strategies in cultural policy and overseas expansion. From 1997 to 2002, the first stage in the Korean wave, as the scale of South Korean cultural industries grew rapidly from 5.4 trillion to 18 trillion won, South Korean cultural policy and cultural industries focused on the Japanese market (Samsung Economic Research Institute 2002).

The size of the Japanese market was seen as the best opportunity for achieving market balance since the liberalization of Japanese popular culture began. According to a 2000 report by Samsung Economic Research Institute, in 1999, the Japanese cinema market was worth 1.828 hundred billion yen. A mere 0.3 percent share of that market would offset the South Korean cinema market's loss of revenue (up to 5 billion won) from the liberalization of Japanese popular culture (Samsung Economic Research Institute 2000). The Korean wave had made such aspirations achievable, as demonstrated by the success of *Shiri*, which was screened in 1999 at the Tokyo International Film Festival, and attracted an audience of 1.2 million across Japan in 2000. Expansion into the Japanese market was confirmation of the potential for South Korean films to be exported to the world market.

Shiri, which was launched into the Japanese cinema market in 1999 for US$1.3 million, was the lead character that opened the way for the export of South Korean films. Until then, the price of a South Korean film had been several tens of thousands of dollars, at most. In addition to Japan, *Shiri* was sold to twenty countries, including Spain, Russia and Germany, recording a total of $2.3 million in export revenue. This year, *JSA*, which set a new audience record for a South Korean film, was sold to the Japanese market for $2 million, twice that of *Shiri*'s sales price, and the U.S., Germany, France, Taiwan, Hong Kong, Singapore and others are being sounded out as to its export. (*Maeil Business Newspaper* 2001b)

Following *Shiri*'s success, the Korean wave accelerated into Japan in 2004 with the highly popular television series *Winter Sonata*. The advance of South Korean popular culture into Japan dramatically transformed perceptions of South Korean cultural industries, which had hitherto been seen as a cultural weakling in contrast to Japan; and this, in turn, generated new cultural discourses and practices. Of course, the financial benefits of penetrating the Japanese market were not the only factor driving changes in South Korean perceptions of Japan; the Japanese acceptance of South Korean cultural products, and the corresponding changes in Japanese people's appreciation of South Korea fostered a new affinity for Japan among South Koreans, also.

The affinity generated by encountering "the popular" through media culture, and the sense of sharing a mutual modernity on an equal footing, was completely different from the "feeling of closeness" that had previously been invoked to explain the two nations' political and economic relations. If we assume the most critical process in constructing a cultural relationship to be how each side defines the other, then the complex sentiments harbored by South Korean society as a former colony and neighbor of Japan changed rapidly as Japan's appetite for South Korean culture rapidly changed its assessment of South Korea. In other words, as it began to see the global circulation of its cultural commodities, South Korea was able to overturn its self-perception as a cultural weakling in fear of a cultural invasion, which enabled the "discovery of South Korea" in Japan to stimulate a "(re-) discovery of Japan" by South Korea.

Between cultural exchange and a culture war

Seemingly overnight, the Korean wave elevated popular culture to the center of state discourse. With the success of the 2002 World Cup, new political and cultural developments via the internet, and great success by South Korean enterprises such as Samsung, the importance of popular culture as the leading representative of South Korea to the world came to be seen as a matter of national interest. Recognizing the Korean wave as an important source of "soft power," the government took positive measures to maximize its economic and cultural effectiveness by expanding its reach. The June 2003 launch of the Korea Foundation for International Cultural Exchange by the Roh Moo-hyun administration was part of this, heralding "the age of North-East Asia," as was the announcement through its "Policy vision and practical plan for cultural industries" (May 2004) which declared that South Korea had entered "the top five cultural industry nations in the world after the U.S., Japan, Britain and France."

The Roh administration remained forward-looking regarding the liberalization of Japanese popular culture. On a visit to Japan in June 2003, Minister for Culture Lee Chang-dong explained the background to President Roh's announcement of further liberalization:

> Results of minute analysis of the influence upon our culture of the three stages of "liberalization of Japanese popular culture" that have been carried out up to now show that the impact from liberalization of Japanese popular culture has been far slighter than was initially feared, and, if anything, it has been an opportunity to raise the competitiveness of our cultural industries, while communicating with diverse cultures. For example, between the liberalization of Japanese popular culture and now, seventy-seven films from our country have been exported to Japan, and Japan is on the way to becoming the major export destination for our domestically-made films. Seen overall, I think it has eufunction rather than dysfunction. (*Yonhap News* 2003)

This was the precursor to the fourth stage of liberalization, commencing January 1, 2004, and breaking the hiatus that had continued since 2000. Among some concerns that South Korean society had effectively accepted "total liberalization," the reactions of the market and public opinion were mixed: the share price for South Korean anime and music companies rose by four to six percent, while film company shares fell by two to three percent (*The Hankyoreh* 2003). Already, events and exchanges were taking place across a variety of domains, and with Japanese popular culture being accepted in everyday life, there were no moves to stir-up the public's apprehension and sense of danger regarding Japanese popular culture. Indeed, there was an upswell of voices welcoming the opportunity for South Korean cultural industries to discard the imitation and plagiarism of Japanese popular culture and thus enhance the competitiveness of South Korean content. If Japanese popular culture in the age of prohibition was both a target of exclusion and an object of negation for South Korean society, in the age of exchange it had become both an object of acceptance and a target of competition. Any legitimacy of the ban on Japanese popular culture had vanished.

The Cool Japan policy, which promoted content industries as a pillar of state strategy, contributed significantly to this turn. As can be seen from the following passage, the competition between Japanese and South Korean culture industries gained momentum from this point.

In South Korea and China, for example, they aim for growth in this field as state policy, commit large amounts of public funds and develop measures, and in some fields, they are seen to have already even gathered sufficient strength to surpass Japan. In Western countries, a taxation system that encourages investment in production; positive assistance towards international film festivals, and, furthermore, active policies by the state in human-resource development and so forth are implemented, and as a result, in these countries, good-quality content is produced, and as a business they are expanding overseas on a large scale... We must promptly and actively expand radical measures for that purpose, positioning the promotion of content industries as the pillar of our national strategy, commencing with legal responses such as these, in order to aim for increased overseas understanding of Japan through the transmission of Japanese culture, in addition to outdoing other countries in competition. (*Chiteki zaisan senryaku honbu kontentsu senmon chōsakai* [Intellectual Property Strategy Headquarters of Japan] 2004: 2–3)

Nevertheless, in 2004 – despite *Winter Sonata*, its young star Bae Yong-joon, and associated merchandise having earned an estimated three trillion won in foreign markets – the South Korean cultural industries began to feel a strong sense of impending crisis. Doubts were raised as to the sustainability of the Korean wave which had continued to swell since 2000. The Asian market's discomfort about the unilateral increase of exports, the weak foundations of domestic cultural industries, and uniformity of content were identified as the main problems (Hyundai Research Institute 2004).

At the same time, numerous questions were raised about the Korean wave and its direction. Among these were expressions of anxiety about the direction the culture was heading since neo-liberalism had become the governing ideology in the wake of the 1997 financial crisis. These were, of course, questions about the nature of South Korean culture, but also about its relations with East Asia, including Japan.

Amid criticism that the Korean wave has recently been very attached solely to Korean wave stars' popularity and business, that wave has weakened. By overlooking the importance of true cultural exchange and being bent on enlarging the scale of economic cultural exchange by means of logic and functional handling, it is a situation where the driving force of the Korean wave is dwindling... The logic of capital is thoroughly taking the initiative in the twenty-first-century cultural network incorporating South Korea and East Asia... Our aims and intentions are certain: "From absence to real existence;" an equal order and true cultural enjoyment hitherto absent from East Asian societies; peace in North-East Asia and the world; each country's firm hold on cultural diversity and the mutual cultural standards and success it generates; and the actual cultural planning. It means properly building a pathway of multidimensional, equitable cultural communication and solidarity that is neither the pervasion of American cultural hegemony, nor a twenty-first-century inversion of Chinese civilization's order of civilized versus uncivilized, or of achievement and the tributary system. (*Hankyoreh 21* 2004)

Japan–South Korea relations were standing at the crossroads between a "clash of soft power" spearheaded by state and capital in one direction, and "cultural cooperation" that was irreducible to the logic of state and capital, in the other. Then, 2005 marked forty years since the normalization of diplomatic relations between Japan and the Republic of Korea. The Japanese and South Korean governments designated 2005 as the "Year of Japan–South Korea Friendship." Had the early twenty-first-century Japan–South Korea relationship transcended the 1965 system? The decade that would answer this question had already dawned.

C onclusion

CAN THE "MECHANISM OF PROHIBITION" BE SURMOUNTED?

The significance of the ban on Japanese popular culture

From the beginning of the 1990s, *Ujusonyeon Atom* (*Astro Boy*) vanished from the skies of South Korea. In his place, the original Japanese *Tetsuwan Atomu* was formally distributed, trans-bordering to South Korea, after it was no longer necessary to deny *Astro Boy*'s nationality. In fact, that denial had become impossible with globalization.

However, this does not imply that the shift in Japan–South Korea relations went so far as to erase people's memories and feelings about *Ujusonyeon Atom*. Children's experiences of comics and television from the 1960s to the 1980s had been of *Ujusonyeon Atom*, not *Tetsuwan Atomu*, and to negate those experiences would mean wholly disaffirming and obliterating the memories of many people. In other words, as I remarked in the Introduction, the narrative around *Ujusonyeon Atom* is not a simple occurrence that could be forgotten without consequence, but one whose structural and historical exploration provides important insights into not only cultural relations between postwar Japan and South Korea, but also South Korean modernity itself.

As such, in apprehending the universality and specificity inherent in the ban on Japanese popular culture, and after further consideration of these along with various geopolitical, economic and social conditions, the question that should be posed is: what was the cultural efficacy of this ban which was in place for several decades? Addressing this question may help to clarify the present relations between the two nations, and to anticipate future issues. I will now endeavor to

176

summarize the problem-consciousness examined in this volume and the character of the ban on Japanese popular culture.

The ban on Japanese popular culture as "power"

The most critical factor in the ban on Japanese popular culture was obviously the Other that was "Japan." As explained in Chapter One, the ban on Japanese popular culture after liberation was an act of identity politics aimed at cultural liberation from Japan – that is, a rejection of its various violently suppressive controls and restraints upon Korean culture. However, this task of decolonization was an historical construct in which multiple justifications conflicted with and contradicted one another in the context of industrial modernization during the Cold War and the reconstruction of Japan–South Korea relations, centered on their mutual relations with the United States. Decolonization was a multilayered process with multiple justifications, including: 1) initial rejection of the cultural influence of the former colonizer (decolonization); 2) local resistance to the globalization of mass media (critique of cultural imperialism); 3) the economic strategy and development of a newly independent nation (industrial modernization); and 4) the multilayered exercise of power through public and private censorship (nationalization).

Practices in the urban media space and the social consciousness connected with them, as discussed in this book, formulated and sustained the ban on Japanese popular culture amid the complex contradictions and conflicts between these four justifications.

As the South Korean popular culture industry grew, Japanese popular culture came to be seen as a new form of cultural encroachment rather than merely the residue of the colonial period, but at the same time the South Korean popular culture industry, recognizing Japanese popular culture as a product of the same model of capitalism that it was trying to emulate, pursued economic development not by excluding Japanese culture, but by disguising its nationality while actively imitating and plagiarizing it (the justification of industrial modernization).

177

The common thread running through these multiple justifications was a "mechanism of negation." As discussed in Part Two, the circulation of much Japanese cultural content – mainly through television broadcasting – merely by removing, disguising or rearranging elements deemed to be "*waesaek*," including Japanese language, Japanese clothing and background scenery, was simultaneously a way of implementing a ban and enabling inflow through a mechanism of negation.

However, this mechanism of negation had an enormous influence on South Koreans' consciousness, not only on the practices in the cultural industries but also on the level of a "structure of feeling" (Williams 2001: 64–65) deeply and widely experienced by South Korean society. Problematizing media practices and mass consumption in the absence of a legal system, with the tacit approval of the state, and fueling a collectively shared anxiety and sense of crisis over these issues, constituted a critical axis which discursively constructed the ban on Japanese popular culture. If the crucial role of the ban was to share perceptions and sentiments within South Korea vis-à-vis the circulation and consumption of Japanese popular culture, it could be argued that through a mechanism of negation in the discursive space, the ban on Japanese popular culture was an exercise of power (Foucault 1978) that permeated everyday behavior and awareness. This occurred because the consumption of Japanese popular culture, which had become an everyday occurrence due to its constant trans-bordering in the absence of stringent exclusionary measures, had become an object of problematization through the discourse of prohibition.

Departure from the mechanism of prohibition

Why, then, was such "negation" possible? The answer can be grasped from the fourth justification, namely that of "nationalization."

As I have reiterated throughout this volume, considering that the trans-bordering by Japanese popular culture coincided with the diffusion of American media and popular culture by the U.S. military, as well as the introduction of capitalist modernization, it was clearly impossible to simply identify and effectively ban "Japanese" products and influences. In that context, people who desired a new modernity enjoyed a complex mixture of American and Japanese popular culture in their everyday lives, and proceeded to reproduce a capitalist culture modelled upon it. As industrial modernization progressed and the middle class grew, that desire continually expanded and materialized through all urban media spaces. Defining the behavior of individual cultural producers and consumers as "breaches" of the ban on Japanese popular culture, sought to mobilize individuals as subconsciously defined "Korean nationals." Thus, satisfying an individual's desire for the "modernity" inherent in Japanese popular culture meant "negating" their status as "nationals" of the Republic of Korea.

Thus, it was not on the basis of decolonization, but rather the stronger basis of "nationalization" interwoven with an "anti-communist" policy, that the dictatorship which had developed robust political and economic ties to Japan espoused an "anti-Japanese" policy and exploited the ban on Japanese popular culture as a means of political censorship. Of course, the formation of "nationals" is a vital process in "decolonization," but what I mean by "nationals" here is something defined, mobilized and constructed by the developmental dictatorship of the 1960s to 1980s. The "mechanism of negation" was possible because the focus of the ban shifted from the initial "identity politics" to the benefit of "nationals" under the developmental dictatorship.

Moreover, the process of imposing this ban on Japanese popular culture ultimately produced two reversals in South Korean society with respect to the agents and targets of prohibition. The first of these was a reversal on the level of practice, in that while on the one hand Japanese popular culture was actively circulating and being consumed within South Korea, South Korean popular culture was being censored to remove any traces of "*waesaek*," and sometimes it was excluded (banned) by external entities; while the second was a "reversal on a spiritual level" in which the people of South Korea, who ought to have been the *agents* of prohibition aimed at cultural liberation from Japan in the "liberation space" – ridding themselves of the violent suppression and restraint of the colonial period – conversely became the *targets* of public and private censorship by means of prohibitions. If we deem "decolonization" to be the gaining of freedom from an Other by repositioning that Other (the former colonizer) as an equal, then, the bans interwoven with "nationalization" produced excess awareness of the Other.

In this context, rather than any changes in cultural policy or the cultural industries, the greatest significance of dismantling the ban on Japanese popular culture from the late 1980s, as discussed in Part Three, could be said to lie in the emergence of an "I" that declared: "I love all popular culture that I have enjoyed, whether it be American or Japanese", as in Yoo Ha's poem cited in Chapter Six – in other words, an agent who rejected the frame of the "negating agent = a national." Moreover, departing from the ban on Japanese popular culture meant breaking free from the mechanism of prohibition that existed unconsciously as "public and private censorship = discursive power," without denying Koreans' persistent desires for mutual connections with the Other. Moreover, it might be seen as a new "decolonization" from the culture that had persisted throughout the former Japanese Empire, as well as through the U.S. military government and Korean military dictatorships.

A reconsideration of the Japan–South Korea cultural relationship

The South Korean negation of Japan was not merely limited to the domestic realm. It also shaped postwar relations between Japan and South Korea, especially the cultural construct of the 1965 system, while resonating with a type of negation by postwar Japanese society in regard to South Korea.

In political terms, Japan's re-encounter with South Korea came after the normalization of diplomatic relations between Japan and the Republic of Korea, and their dispute over the 1965 treaty, while economically it was after the expansion of international markets, and the relocation of a cheap labor force and polluting industries to Korea (Yoon 2003: 290), but Japan's interest in South Korean culture only began in the 1990s, when it realized the economic value of trading (Iwabuchi ed. 2003) Japanese cultural products in the Asian region, including South Korea; and it was not until the early twenty-first century that Japan began to positively engage in a cultural relationship with South Korea, in the wake of the so-called Korean wave.

Until then, Japan had arguably continued to objectify South Korea as "the Other beyond the border," with connections limited to political and economic concerns at a state level, rather than an Other that had once been subsumed within Japan, or a near neighbor. As many scholars have argued, at the root of this "Othering" lay a deep-seated ignorance and indifference towards the people of the former colony. While the people in post-independence South Korea were "excessively" conscious of the Other that was Japan, in postwar Japan, the Other that was South Korea tended to be "absent." Might this dialectic between an "excess of the Other" and an "absence of the Other" be the crux for explaining Japan–South Korea cultural relations in the postwar?

If we assume that the twentieth-century Japan–South Korea relationship was built upon the colonial system and the 1965 system, then Japan and South Korea spent that century without once facing each other squarely on the level of official history, as if on an (un)conscious level, they continued to deny each other's existence. Within the vast frame of the Cold War, although both nations aligned with America and experienced rapid development and growth, the postcolonial cultural relationship between Japan and South Korea avoided acknowledging or addressing a variety of problems inherent in their mutual present, and has thus not yet fully escaped the 1965 system.

If that is the case, despite Japan and South Korea's having developed an unprecedented mutual affinity through cultural exchange at the dawn of the twenty-first century, how can we understand the relationship between the two countries of today, which in the 2010s suddenly brimmed with unprecedented enmity? Does the violent clash between those feelings of affinity and enmity represent labor pains necessary for Japan and South Korea to shake off the 1965 system and face each other freely; or is it the beginning of a fresh "mechanism of prohibition" for renewed negation of the Other that they have already confronted since the start of the twenty-first century?

Bibliography

Aoki, Shin, 2013, *Meguriau monotachi no gunzō: sengo Nihon no beigun kichi to ongaku 1945-1958* (A lively bunch that chanced to meet: U.S. military bases in postwar Japan and music, 1945-1958), Ōtsuki Shoten.

Appadurai, Arjun, 1990, *Modernity at Large: Global Dimension of Globalization*, Minneapolis: University of Minnesota Press.

Arrighi, Giovanni, 1994, *The Long Twentieth Century: Money, Power, and the Origins of Our Time*, London and New York: Verso.

Barbrook, Richard, 1992, 'Broadcasting and national identity in Ireland,' *Media, Culture & Society*, 14.2: 203–227.

Barker, Chris, 1997, *Global Television: An introduction*, Oxford: Blackwell.

Barth, Fredrik, 1969, *Ethnic Groups and Boundaries: The Social Organization of Culture Difference*, Boston: Little, Brown and Company.

Bataillem, George, 1957, *L'erotisme*, Paris: Minuit (trans. Sakai Ken, 2004, *Erotishizumu* (Eroticism), Chikuma Shobō).

Bhabha, Homi K. 1990, 'Introduction: Narrating the Nation,' in Homi K. Bhabha (ed.), *Nation and Narration*, London: Routledge, 1–7.

——— 1994, *The Location of Culture*, London and New York: Routledge.

Bureau of Judicial Affairs of South Korea, 1968, 'Question regarding exhibition of Japanese cultural films,' Gov. doc. 1740–8748, ROK National Records Center materials, 16 July 1968.

Buck–Morss, Susan, 2002, *Dreamworld and Catastrophe*, Cambridge, MA: MIT Press.

Busan Japanese School, 1981, *Shōwa 56-nendo Busan Nihonjin gakkō yōran* (1981–82 School Handbook of Busan Japanese School), Busan Japanese School.

——— 1984, *Shōwa 59-nendo Busan Nihonjin gakkō yōran* (1984–85 School Handbook of Busan Japanese School), Busan Japanese School.

Busan Munhwa Broadcasting Corporation, 2009, *A 50-year History of Busan munhwa broadcasting*, Busan Munhwa Broadcasting Corporation.

Butler, Judith, 1990, *Gender Trouble: Feminism and the Subversion of Identity*, New York and London: Routledge.

Cho, Hang je, 1994, *1970 nyeondae hangung tellebijeonui gujojeong seonggyeoge gwanhan yeongu* (A study on the structural characteristics of Korean television in the 1970s), PhD Dissertation, Seoul National University.

——— 2008, *Hanguk bangsongui yulliwa yeoksa* (Ethics and history of Korean broadcasting), Nonhyeon.

Cho, Hee-yeon, 2010, *Dongwondoen geundaehwa* (Mobilized modernization), Humanitas.

Chohan, Haejoang, 2003, Geullobeol jigang byeondongui jinghuro ingneun hallyu yeolpung (The Hallyu craze read as a sign of global tectonic change), in Chohan, H. et al. (ed.), *Hallyuwa asiaui daejungmunhwa* (Hallyu and Asian pop culture), Seoul: Yonsei University Press, 1–42.

Choi, Changbong, 1985, OegukTVga hangung TVe kkichin yeonghyang, Kim (The influence of foreign TV on Korean TV), Woo-chang et al. (eds.), *Uri munhwaui jindangwa banseong*, Seoul: Munyegisulsa, 365–373.

Choi, In-hoon, 2002, 'Mwŏl irŭshin ke ŏpsŭshimnikka? (Aren't you forgetting something?),' *T'ainŭi pang* (Another person's room), Munhakdongne.

Choi, Jun, 1963, "Ilbonsangp'umgwanggoŭi ch'imt'ue" (Penetration of Japanese product advertising), *The Sasanggae*, No.122, June 1963: 172–176.

Cohen, Robin, 1994, *Frontiers of Identity: The British and the others*, London: Longman.

Collins, Richard, 1990, *Culture, Communication, and National Identity: The case of Canadian television*, Toronto: University of Toronto Press.

Cumings, Bruce, 1981, *The Origins of the Korean War*, Princeton, New York: Princeton University Press.

Donnan, Hastings and Thomas M. Wilson, 1999, *Borders: Frontiers of Identity, Nation and State*, Oxford: Berg.

Douglas, Mary, 2003, *Purity and Danger: An Analysis of Concepts of Pollution and Taboo*, London: Taylor & Francis. (trans. Tsukamoto Toshiaki, 2009, *Kegare to kinki* (Pollution and taboo), Chikuma Shobō).

Durkeim, Emile, 1912, *Les formes élémentaires de la vie religieuse: Le système totémique en Australie*, Paris: Les Presses universitaires de France (trans. Furuno Kiyoto, 1941, *Shūkyō seikatsu no genshi keitai* (The elementary forms of religious life), Iwanami Bunko.

—— 1925, *L'Education Morale*, Paris: Librairie Felix Alcan (trans. Asō Makoto and Yamamura Takeshi, 2000, *Dōtoku kyōiku ron* (On moral education), Kōdansha.

Edensor, Tim, 2002, *National Identity: Popular Culture and Everyday Life*, Oxford: Berg.

Featherstone, Mike, 1991, *Consumer Culture and Postmodernism*, London and Newbury Park, Calif.: Sage

Film Promotion Committee, 2000, *Summary of the 3rd Opening of Japanese Popular Culture*.

Foucault, Michel, 1978, *The History of Sexuality. Volume I: An Introduction*, (trans. from French by Robert Hurley), New York: Random House.

—— 1988, 'Technologies of the self,' in Luther H. Martin, Huck Gutman and Patrick H. Hutton (eds.), *Technologies of the Self: A seminar with Michel Foucault*, Amherst: University of Massachusetts Press: 16–49.

Foundation for Broadcast Culture, 2005, *Bangsonginyeomeuroseoui gongik-gaenyeomui hyeongseonggwa geonjeonhan gungminui hyeongseong: dongwonhyeonggukgajuuireul jungsimeuro* (Formation of the concept of public interest as a broadcasting ideology and the formation of a healthy nation-focused on mobilization-type nationalism), Foundation for Broadcast Culture.

—— 2007a, *Haebangihu hangukbangsongui hyeongseonge gwanhan gusurye-ongu: Choi, Chang–bong* (Oral study on the formation of Korean broadcasting after liberation), Foundation for Broadcast Culture.

—— 2007b, *Haebangihu hangukbangsongui hyeongseonge gwanhan gusurye-ongu: Jeon Eung–deok* (Oral study on the formation of Korean broadcasting after liberation), Foundation for Broadcast Culture.

—— 2007c, *Haebangihu hangukbangsongui hyeongseonge gwanhan gusurye-ongu: Hwang Jeong–tae* (Oral study on the formation of Korean broadcasting after liberation), Foundation for Broadcast Culture.

Freud, Sigmund, 1991, (trans. J. Strachey), *Introductory Lectures on Psychoanalysis*, London: Penguin.

—— 2001, (trans. J. Strachey), 'Totem and Taboo,' *The Standard Edition of the Complete Psychological Works of Sigmund Freud Volume XIII (1913–1914)*, Vintage, 1–162.

—— 2003, 'On the Introduction of Narcissism,' (trans. J. Reddick), *The Penguin Freud Reader*, London: Penguin, 3–30.

—— 2005, 'Negation,' (trans. G. Frankland), *The Unconscious*, London: Penguin, 87–92.

—— 2006, (trans. J. A. Underwood,), *Interpreting Dreams*, Penguin.

Giddens, Anthony, 1985, *The Nation–State and Violence*, Cambridge: Polity Press.

Gillespie, Marie, 1995, *Television, Ethnicity and Cultural Change*, New York: Routledge.

Goldstein, Robert J., 1989, *Political Censorship of the Arts and the Press in Nineteenth–Century Europe*, London: Macmillan Press.

Hall, Stuart, 1992, 'The Question of Cultural Identity,' in Stuart Hall, David Held and Anthony McGrew (eds.), *Modernity and Its Futures*, Oxford: Blackwell, 273–316.

Han, Seungheon, 1994, *Jeongbohwa sidaeui jeojakgwon* (Copyright in the Information Age), Seoul: Nanam.

Held, David, Anthony McGrew, David Goldblatt, and Jonathan Perraton, 1999, *Global Transformation: Politics, Economics and Culture*. Stanford, CA: Stanford University Press.

Hu, Kelly, 2003, 'Saisōzō sareru nihon no terebi dorama: chūgokugoken ni okeru kaizokuban VCD (Recreated Japanese television dramas: Pirated VCD versions in the Sinophone world),' in Iwabuchi, Koichi, (ed.) *Gurōbaru purizumu: "Ajian dorīmu" toshite no nihon no terebi dorama* (Global prism: Japanese television dramas as an "Asian dream"), Heibonsha, 100-126.

Hyundai Research Institute 2004, *The Korean wave phenomenon and strategy to turn it into a cultural industry.*

Hutcheon, Linda, 1989, 'Circling the Downspout of Empire: Post–Colonialism and Postmodernism,' ARIEL: *A Review of International English Literature*, 20.4: 149–175.

Intellectual Property Strategy Headquarters of Japan, 2004, *Contents-business promotion policy: state strategy in an age of soft power*, April 2004 issue.

Iwabuchi, Koichi, 2002, *Recentering Globalization: Popular Culture and Japanese Transnationalism*, Durham, NC: Duke University Press.

—— (ed.), 2003, *Gurōbaru purizumu: "Ajian dorīmu" toshite no Nihon no terebi dorama* (Global prism: Japanese television dramas as an "Asian dream"), Heibonsha.

Japanese National Diet, 1988, *Record of Proceedings of the Education Committee (House of Representatives)*, No. 10.

Jeon, Jaeho, 1998, 'Minjokjuuiwa yeoksaui iyong: Park Chung-hee chejeui jeontongmunhwajeongchaek (Nationalism and the use of history: Park Chung-hee's traditional culture policy),' *Sahoegwahagyeongu* (Social science research), 7: 83–106.

—— 2002, 'Hangung minjokjuuiwa banil (Korean nationalism and anti-Japanese),' *Jeongchibipyeong* (Political criticism), 2: 128–148.

Jeon, Seokho, 1990, 'Bidio suyongseongui yeongu gwajewa jeonmang (Research challenges and prospects for video receptivity),' *Jeongbosahoeyeongu* (Information Society Research), Fall, 46–75.

Jeon, Yungpyo, 1993, *Jeongbosahoewa jeojakgwon: Jisik jeongboui gukjeyutong* (Information Society and Copyright – International Distribution of Knowledge and Information and Intellectual Property), Beopgyeong.

Jeong, Jonghyun, 2009, Jayuwa minju, singminji yulli gamg: Jeong BiSeok soseoreul tonghae bon migung hegemoniha hangungmunhwa jaepyeonui jendeojeongchihak (Recontextualization of freedom, democracy, and colonial ethical senses: Gender politics of reorganizing Korean culture under hegemony in the United States through Jeong Biseok's novel), in Kwon, B. et al (eds.), *Aphuleykel sasanggyereul ikda: 1950 nyeondae munhwaui* (Reading Apres girl thoughts: Freedom and control of culture in the 1950s), Gyeongju: Dongkook University Press.

Kang, Sangjung and Hyun, Mooam, 2010, *Dainippon/Manshū teikoku no isan* (The legacy of the Great Japanese/Manchurian empire), Kōdansha.

Kang, Jun-man, 2003, *Hangukyeondaesa sanchaek: 1980nyeondaepyeon je 1 gwon* (A walk in contemporary Korean history – Volume 1 of the 1980s), Inmulgwa sasangsa.

—— 2004, *Hangukyeondaesa sanchaek: 1960nyeondaepyeon je 2 gwon* (A walk in contemporary Korean history – Volume 2 of the 1960s), Inmulgwa sasangsa.

Kang. Myung-koo, 1994, Gukjehwawa munhwajeong minjujuui (International-ization and cultural democracy), *Changjakgwa bipyeong* (Creation and criticism), 22: 70–87.

Kano, Kiyoko, and Tsuchiya Takeshi, 2002, 'Nikkan rekishi kyōkasho mondai no kadai to tenbō (The issue of history textbooks in Japan and Korea, and its prospects),' *Aichi Kyōiku Daigaku Kyōiku Jissen Sōgō Sent⊠ Kiyō*, Aichi University of Education, 5: 25-32.

Katz, Elihu, and George Wedell, 1977, *Broadcasting in the Third World*, Cambridge, MA: Harvard University.

Katzenstein, Peter J., 2005. *A World of Regions: Asia and Europe in the American Imperium*, Ithaca, N.Y.: Cornell University Press.

Kim. Changnam, 2003, *Daejungmunhwaui ihae* (Understanding popular culture), Hanul akademi.

Kim. Dongchul, 1995, 'Urinaraui bangsongbeobui byeoncheongwajeong (Changes in broadcasting law in Korea),' *Bangsongyeongu* (Broadcasting research), 2–25.

Kim, Dongchun, 2000, *Geundaeui Geuneul* (Shadow of modern history), Dolbegae.

Kim, Dukho, 2008, 'Hangugeseoui ilsangsaenghwalgwa sobiui migukwa munje (The Americanization of daily life and consumption in Korea),' in Kim, D. and Won, Y. (eds), *Americanization: Haebang ihu hangugeseoui migukwa* (Americanization: Americanization in Korea after liberation), Pureunyeoksa, 122–158.

Kim, Hakjae, 2011, 'Jeongbusurim jeonhu gongbobucheoui hwaldonggwa naengjeontongchiseongui gyebo (Activities of the public affairs department before and after the establishment of the government and the genealogy of Cold War rules),' *Daedongmunhwayeongu* (Daedong culture research), 74: 61–97.

Kim, Jueon, 1989, '80 nyeondae eollontanap (Media oppression in the 80s),' *Sahoepyeongnon* (Social commentary), 3: 154–198.

Kim, Moonjo and Park, Sooho, 1998, 'Hangugui munhwajeongchaek: Hoegowa jeonmang (Korea's cultural policy: Retrospective and prospects),' *Aseayeongu* (Asia research), 40: 297–323.

Kim, Sungmin, 2009, 'Rōkaru na kinshi to gurōbaruka no rikigaku: 1980-nendai Kankoku ni okeru Nihon taishū bunka kinshi to kokusai chosakuken mondai (Dynamics between the Local Ban and Globalization: Influences of the International Copyright Law on the Ban on Japanese Popular Culture in Korea in the 1980s),' *The Annual Review of Sociology* (Japan), 22: 103–113.

―――― 2010, 'Kinshi to ekkyō: gojū~nanajū nendai Kankoku Pusan ni okeru Nihon no denpa ekkyō' (The Ban and Spill-over: The Cultural Meanings of Broadcast Spill-over from Japan in Busan, Korea in the 1950–1970s),' *Journal of Mass Communication Studies* (Japan), 76: 237–254.

―――― 2011, "Bunkateki kokkyō to sōzō sareta kinshi: gojū~rokujū nendai Kankoku taishū bunka ni okeru washoku no bunka seiji (Cultural border and imagined ban: Cultural politics of waesek in South Korea during the 1950s and 1960s)", *Journal of Information Studies*, Tokyo University, 81: 1-22.

―――― 2013, *Kinshi to yokubō: rokujū~hachijū nendai kaihatsu dokusaiki Kankoku ni okeru Nihon taishū bunka no ekkyō* (Bans and Desire: Transnational Flows of Japanese Popular Culture in South Korea during the 1960s and 1980s), PhD dissertation, Interdisciplinary Informatics, Graduate School, the University of Tokyo.

―――― 2014, 'Tsurumi Shunsuke to Kankoku no bunka shakaigaku (Tsurumi Shunsuke and cultural sociology in South Korea),' in Yoshimi Shunya (ed.) *Bunka shakaigaku kihon bunkenshū bekkan* (Basic compilation of sources [in] cultural sociology, separate volume), Nihon Tosho Sentā, 179–207.

Kim, Yoontae, 1999, 'Baljeongukgaui giwongwa seongjang: Rhee syng-man gwa Park Chung-hee gwanhan yeoksasahoehakjeong yeongu (The origin and growth of the developing nation: A historical and sociological study on Syng-man Rhee and Chung-hee Park),' *Sahoewa yeoksa* (Society and history), 56: 145–177.

Kim, Yerim, 2007a, '1960 nyeondae junghuban gaebal naesyeoneollijeumgwa jungsancheun (Cultural politics of nationalism and middle-class family fantasy in the mid-late 1960s),' *Hyeondaemunhagyeongu* (Contemporary literature studies), 32: 339–375.

―――― 2007b, 'Naengjeongi asia sangsanggwa bangong jeongcheseongui wisanghak: Gaebang-hangukjeonjaenghu (1945~1955), asia simsangjirireul jungsimeuro (The Cold War Asian imagination and the topology of anti-communist identity: Openness to post-Korean War (1945–1955), focusing on Asian image geography),' Sangheohakbo (Journal of modern Korean literature), 20: 311–345.

Ko, Un, 2006, *Ten Thousand Lives: 21, 22, 23*, Changbi.

Koo, Kwang-mo, 1998, 'Urinara munhwajeongchaegui mokpyowa teukseong: 80 nyeondaewa 90 nyeondaereul jungsimeuro (Goals and characteristics of cultural policy in Korea: Focused on the 1980s and 1990s),' *Junganghaengjeongnonjip* (Central Administrative Papers), 12: 1–17.

Korea Cultural Policy Development Institute, 1994, *Study on the Plan for Response to Open to Japanese Popular Culture.*

Korea Culture and Tourism Policy Institute, 2003, *Analysis of the Influence of Liberalization of Japanese Popular Culture and Plan of Response.*

Laplanche, Daniel, and Jean-Bertrand Pontalis, 1967, *Vocabulaire de la psychanalyse*, Paris: PUF (sup. trans. Murakami Masashi, 1977, *Seishin bunseki yōgo jiten* (Dictionary of psychoanalytic terms), Misuzu Shobō).

Lee, Bong-beom, 2008a, '1950 nyeondae munhwajaepyeongwa geomyeol (Cultural restructure and censorship in 1950s),' *Hangungmunha gyeongu* (Korean literature studies), 34: 7–49.

―――― 2009, '1950 nyeondae munhwajeongchaekgwa yeonghwageomyeol (Cultural policy and film censorship in the 1950s),' *Hangungmunha gyeongu* (Korean literature studies), 37: 409–467.

Lee, Dongyeon, 2008b, 'Singminji naemyeonhwawa naengjeongi cheongnyeonjucheui hyeongseong (Colonial internalization and the formation of youth in Cold War period: A study on the specificity of youth culture in the 1945–50s),' in Institute for East Asian Studies at Sungkonghoe University (eds.), *Naengjeonasiaui munhwapunggyeong 1: 1940–50 nyeondae* (Asian cultural landscape in Cold War 1, 1940–50s), Hyeonsilmunhwa: 385–407.

Lee, Kangro, 2004, Hangung nae banmijuuiui seongjanggwajeong bunseok (Analysis of the growth process of anti-Americanism in Korea), *Gukjejeongchinonjip* (International politics), 44(4): 239–261.

Lee, Kihyung, 2005, 'Taljiyeokjeogeuro suyongdoeneun daejungmunhwaui busanggwa hallyuhyeon (The rise of popular culture accepted non-regional and cultural politics surrounding the Korean Wave phenomenon),' *Eollongwa sahoe* (media and society), 13(2): 189–213.

Lee, Okkyung, 1984, '70 nyeondae daejungmunhwa (Characteristics of popular culture in the 70s),' *Yeoksawa gidokgyo* (History and christianity), Minjungsa.

Lee, Sungwook, 2004, *Shoshosho, Gimchuja, seondeiseoul, gedaga gingeupjochi* (Show Show Show Kim Chuja, Sunday Seoul, and Emergency rule), Saenggagui namu.

Lee, Sunmi, 2006, 'Migugeul sobihaneun daedosiwa migugyeonghwa: 1950 nyeondae hangugui migugyeonghwa sangyeonggwa gwallamui uimi 1 (Big cities and American films consuming the United States: The meaning of screening and watching American films in Korea in the 1950s),' in Sangheohakoe (eds.), *1950 nyeondae midieowa miguk*, (1950s Media and American Representation), Gipeunsaem, 73–105.

—— 2009, '1950 nyeondae migung yuhakgwa daehangmunhwa: Yeonhuichunchuui migukgwallyeon damnongwa gisareul jungsimeuro (Studying in the United States and University Culture in the 1950s: Focused on the discourses and articles related to the United States),' *Sangheohakbo* (Journal of modern Korean literature), 25: 235–272.

Lee, Soonjin, 2010, 'Hangukjeonjaeng hu naengjeonui nolliwa singminji gieogui jaeguseong: 1950 nyeondae munhwayeonghwaeseo guchukdoen iseungman seosareul jungsimeuro (The logic of the Cold War After the Korean War and the reconstruction of colonial memory: Focused on 'The Syngman Rhee Narrative' constructed from cultural films in the 1950s),' *Gieokgwa jeonmang* (Memory and vision), 23: 70–103.

Lee, Youngmi, 1998, *Hangukdaejungeumaksa,*(Popular music history in Korea), Sigongsa.

—— 2002, *Heungnambuduui geumsunineun eodiro gasseulkka* (Where did Geum-soon of Heungnam Pier go?), Hwanggeumgaji.

Lévi–Strauss, Claude, 1942, *Les Structures élémentaires de la Parenté*, Mouton & Co.: Maison des Science de l'Homme (trans. Fukui Kazumi, 2001, *Shinzoku no kihon kōzō* (The elementary forms of kinship), Seikyūsha.

Lim, Jihyun, 2000, 'Hanbando minjokjuuiwa gwollyeokdamnon: Bigyosajeong munjejegi (Nationalism and power discourse on the Korean peninsula – Raising comparative issues),' *Dangdaebipyeong* (Contemporary criticism), 10: 183–206.

Lim, Jongsoo, 2004, Hangukbangsongui giwon: chogi radio bangsongeseo jedo, pyeonseong, jangneuui hyeongseonggwa jinhwa (The origin of Korean broadcasting: Formation and evolution of institution, programming, genre in the early radio age), *Hangugeollonhakbo* (Korean journal of journalism), 48–6: 370–396.

Ministry of Culture and Sports of South Korea, 1978, 'Korea–Japan Cultural Exchange Plan,' Gov. doc. 750–1244, ROK National Records Center materials, 30 August.

——1994, *Study on the Plan for Response to Japanese Popular Culture*.

Ministry of Culture, Sports, and Tourism of South Korea, 2013, *Hallyu white paper 2013*.

Ministry of Culture and Tourism of South Korea, 1998, *Press Release: Guidelines for phased liberalization of Japanese popular culture*, 21 October 1998.

——2000, *Our promise to open up a cultural century*.

Ministry of Foreign Affairs of Japan, 1998, *Japan–South Korea Joint Declaration: A new Japan–South Korea Partnership aimed at the twenty-first century*, 8 October 1998.

Ministry of Home Affairs of South Korea, 1971, 'Question regarding trademarks and designation of contents in merchandise advertisements,' Gov. doc. 2032.3.-4264, BA0136835, "ROK National Records Center" materials, 7 June 1971.

Ministry of Culture and Information of South Korea, 1979, *A 30-year history of culture and information.*

Moon, Katherine H. S., 1997, *Sex Among Allies: Military Prostitution in U.S.– Korea. Relations*, New York: Columbia University Press. (Lee J.(tr.), 2002, *Dongmaeng sogui sekseu*, Samin.)

Moon, Okbae, 2004, *Hangung geumjigogui sahoesa* (Social history of banned songs in Korea), Yesol.

Morisaki, Kazue, 1971, *Izoku no genki* (Principles of otherness), Daiwa Shobō.

Morley, David, and Kevin Robins, 1995, *Space of Identity: Global Media, Electronic Landscapes and Global* Boundaries, London: Routledge. (trans. Ma, D. & Nam, K., 1999, *Bangsongui segyehwawa munhwajeongcheseong*, Hanurakademi.)

Natsume, Fusanosuke, 2003, 'Higashi Ajia ni hirogaru manga bunka (Manga culture that spreads to East Asia),' in Aoki Tamotsu et. al (eds.), *Media: Genron to hyōshō no chiseigaku* (Media: the geopolitics of media discourse and representation), Iwanami Shoten, 179–194.

Oh, Jaekyung, 2003, *Jukpoojaegyeongmunseonjip: Pyeongbeomeul bibeomeuro* (Anthology of Jukpo Ojae Sutras: From ordinary to extraordinary) Jukpoojaegyeongmunseonjim ganhaengwiwonhoe (Jukpo Ojae Gyeongmun Anthology Publishing Committee).

Oh, Myungseok, 1998, '1960–70 nyeondaeui munhwajeongchaekgwa minjong-munhwa damnon (Cultural policy and national culture discourse in the 1960s and 1970s),' *Bigyomunhwayeongu* (Comparative culture research), 4: 121–152.

Office of Public Information of South Korea, 1958, 'Duty Allocation Chart,' January 1958.

Park, Jaeyong, 1993, *Hangung chogi mingan sangeopbangsongui baljeong-wajeonge gwanhan yeongu* (A Study on the Development Process of Early Private Commercial Broadcasting in Korea), MA Dissertation, Seoul National University.

Park, Soon Ae and Tsuchiya Reiko (eds.), 2002, *Nihon taishū bunka to Nikkan kankei: Kankoku wakamono to Nihon imēji* (Japanese popular culture and Japanese–South Korean relations: South Korean youth and the image of Japan), Sangensha.

Publication Ethics Committee, 2000, *Thirty Years of Publication Ethics*, Publication Ethics Committee.

Republic of Korean National Parliament, 1976, *Minutes of the 9th Special Committee for Budget Resolution*, Administrative Agency.

———— 1978, *Minutes of the Culture and Public Information Committee*, 20 October 1978.

———— 1981, *108th Record of Proceedings of the Culture, Education and Public Information Committee*, No. 6: 27.

———— 1986, *Record of Proceedings of the 131st National Assembly Plenary Session*, No. 20, Appendix 2: 545.

Research Center for Cultural Development, 1989, *Study on the Popular Culture Industry and Popular Culture Policy*, South Korean Institute for Culture and Arts Promotion.

Roach, Colleen, 1993, 'American Textbooks vs. NWICO History,' in George Gerbner, Hamid Mowlana, and Kärle Nordenstreng (eds.), *The Global Media Debate: Its Rise, Fall, and Renewal*, New Jersey: Ablex: 35–47.

Roh, Jungpal, 2003, *Hangukbangsonggwa 50 nyeon* (50 Years of Korean Broadcasting), Seoul: Nanam.

Said, Edward, 1993, *Culture and Imperialism*, London: Vintage.

Samsung Economic Research Institute, 2000, *Japanese products are on their way*.

————2002, *Main issues and response strategies to cultural market liberalization*.

Sassen, Saskia, 2006, *Territory, Authority, Rights: From Medieval to Global Assemblages*, Princeton: Princeton University Press.

Schlesinger, Philip, 1987, 'On national identity: Some conceptions and misconceptions,' *Social Science Information*, 26: 219–264.

Schmitt, Carl, 1932, *Der Begriff des Politischen*, Duncker and Humblot: München (trans. Tanaka Hiroshi and Harada Takeo, 1970, *Seijiteki na mono no gainen* (The concept of the political), Miraisha).

Seo, Hyunseok, 2009, *Goemurabeoji peuroiteu: Hwanggeumbakjwiwa yogoeingan* (Freud, the monster father: The golden bat and the monster man), Hannarae.

Shin, Hyunjoon and Ho, Tung-hung, 2008, 'Singminji naemyeonhwawa naengjeongi cheongnyeon jucheui hyeongseong: 1940–50 nyeondae cheongnyeonmunhwaui teugiseong yeongu (Nationalization of popular entertainment in South Korea and Taiwan in the early Cold War, and translation of American popular culture),' in Institute for East Asian Studies at Sungkonghoe University (eds.), *Naengjeonasiaui munhwapunggyeong 1: 1940–50 nyeondae* (Asian cultural landscape in Cold War 1, 1940–50s), Hyeonsilmunhwa: 311–360.

Shin, Ilchul, 1964, 'Munhwajŏng shingminjihwaŭi pangbi-ilbonŭi saekchŏngmunhwarŭl magara (Defense of cultural colonization: Prevent Japan's sexual culture),' *Sasanggae* (World of thought), No. 133, April: 58–61.

Shin, Junghyeon, 2006, *Nae gitaneun jamdeulji anneunda* (My guitar never sleeps), Haeto.

Shiraishi, Saya, 2007, 'Higashi ajia taishū bunka nettowāku to Nikkan bunka kōryū (East Asian popular culture networks and Japanese–South Korean cultural exchange),' in Hamashita Takeshi and Ch'oe Chang-jip (eds.), *Higashi Ajia no naka no Nikkan kōryū* (Japanese–South Korean exchange in East Asia), Keiō Gijuku Daigaku Shuppankai: 49–76.

Smith, Philip, 2001, *Cultural Theory: An Introduction*, Oxford: Blackwell.

Song, Euna, 1999, 'Outlook: Liberalization of Japanese culture and the South Korean advertising world,' *Monthly Advertising Bulletin*, April: 40–44.

Song, Jaegeuk, 1995, 'Bangsonggisurui byeoncheon (Changes in Broadcasting Technology),' *Bangsongyeongu* (Broadcasting research), 19: 127–147.

South Korean Broadcasting Committee, 1992, *Collection of Broadcasting Review Cases,* South Korean Broadcasting Committee.

South Korean Publication Ethics Committee, 1990, *Analysis of a survey of Japanese copied manga and comparison of Korean and Japanese boys' and girls' manga magazines.*

—— 1991, *Research relating to plans for improvement of the distribution pattern of manga in South Korea.*

Stallybrass, Peter, and Allon White, 1986, *The Politics and Poetics of Transgression*, London: Taylor & Francis.

Steiner, Franz, 1956, *Taboo*, London: Cohen & West.

Takasaki, Sōji, 1996, *Kenshō Nikkan kaidan* (An investigation [into] Japan–ROK talks), Iwanami Shoten.

Telecommunications Development Research Institute, 1990, *Research for Expansion of Broadcasting Production,* Telecommunications Development Research Institute.

The 30-year History of Munhwa Broadcasting Corporation Committee, 1992, *A 30-year history of Munhwa broadcasting*, Munhwa Broadcasting Corporation.

The 70-year history of Korean Broadcasting System Committee, 1997, *A 70-year history of Korean broadcasting*, Korean Broadcasting System.

The Government of the Republic of Korea, 1965, The *White Paper on Talks between the Republic of Korea and Japan.*

Tomlinson, 1991, *Cultural Imperialism: A Critical Introduction*, Baltimore: Johns Hopkins University Press.

Tovey, Hilary, and Perry Share, 2000, *A Sociology of Ireland*, Dublin: Gill and Macmillan.

Weber, Max, 1922, *Soziologische Grundbegriffe, „Wirtschaft und Gesellschaft"*, Tübingen: J.C.B. Mohr (trans. Shimizu Ikutarō, 1972, *Shakaigaku no konpon gainen* (Fundamental concepts of sociology), Iwanami Shoten).

—— [1922]1972, 'Grundriß der Verstehenden Soziologie', Wirtschaft und Gesellschaft, Studienausgabe (trans. Sera Terushirō, 1974, *Hōshakaigaku* (Sociology of law), Sōbunsha).

Williams, Chris, 2004, (trans. J. Kim) 'Byeongyeongeseo baraboda: Geundae seoyureobui gukgyeonggwa byeongyeong, Geundaeui gukgyeong yeoksaui byeongyeong: Byeongyeonge seoseo yeoksareul baraboda (On the razor's edge: Understanding borders in modern history),' *Humanist*, 39–71.

Williams, Raymond, 2001, *The Long Revolution*, Peterborough: Broadview Press.

Wilson, Thomas M., and Hastings Donnan, 1998, *Border Identities: Nation and state at international frontiers*, New York: Cambridge University Press.

Yamada Shōji, 2007, *Kaizokuban no shisō: jūhasseiki eikoku no eikyū kopīraito tōsō* (The idea of pirated versions: 18th-century Britain's eternal copyright battle), Misuzu Shobō.

Yeom, Chanhee, 2008, 'Ilsangui jaepyeongwa yongmangui misijeongchihak (Reorganization of daily life and micropolitics of desire),' in Institute for East Asian Studies at Sungkonghoe University (eds.), *Naengjeonasiaui munhwapunggyeong 1: 1940–50 nyeondae* (Asian cultural landscape in Cold War 1, 1940–50s), Hyeonsilmunhwa: 409–457.

Yoo, Byungyong, 1999, 'Park Jung–hee jeongbuwa hanilhyeopjeong (Korea–Japan agreement with the Park Jung-hee government),' in The Academy of Korean Studies (eds.), *1960 nyeondae daeoegwangyewa nambungmunje* (External relations and inter-Korean issues in the 1960s), Baeksanseodang, 11–50.

Yoo, Ha, 1995, *Seunsangga kideuui sarang* (Love of Seun Sangga KIDS), Munhak kwa Chisŏngsa.

Yoo, Sunyoung, 1998, 'Hollun jeongcheseongui yeoksa: Hangung munhwahye-onsang bunseo (The history of single eye identity: Conceptual frame study for analysis of Korean cultural phenomena),' *Hangugeollonhakbo* (Korean journal of journalism), 43: 427–467.

Yoon, Guncha, 2003, *Hanil geundaesasangui gyochak* (Blend of Korean and Japanese modern thoughts), Munhwagwahaksa.

Yoshimi, Shunya, 2002, 'Reisen taisei to Amerika no shōhi: taishū bunka ni okeru sengo no chiseigaku (The cold war system and American consumption: Postwar geopolitics in popular culture),' in Komori Kōichi et. al (eds.), *Reisen taisei to shihon no bunka; 1950-nendai ikō, 1* (The cold war regime and capitalist culture: From the 1950s on, 1), Iwanami Shoten, 3–62.

—— 2007, *Shinbei to hanbei: sengo Nihon no seijiteki muishiki* (Pro-U.S. and anti-U.S.: Postwar Japan's political unconscious), Iwanami Shinsho.

Yun, Kŏn-ch'a, 2008, *Shisō taiken no kōsaku: Nihon, Kankoku, Zainichi 1945 igo* (The intersection of ideological experiences: Japan, South Korea and Japan-residing Koreans after 1945), Iwanami Shoten.

Newspapers, magazines, websites and other primary sources

Asahi Shinbun, 1968, 'Still Banning. Japanese film in Korea,' 1 September.

———— 1988, 'The girls sang a Japanese song that is taboo in Korea,' 19 August.

———— 1998a, 'KAKEHASHI (Japan coming! Korean cultural affairs),' 15 September.

———— 1998b, 'A happy ending for the opening up of Japanese pop culture in Korea,' 14 November.

———— 2001, 'Pro-Japanese? You too,' 19 August.

Bae, Sun-hwan. Interview. Conducted by Kim, Sungmin, 8 Aug. 2008

Chosun Ilbo, 1946, 'What? *Waesaek* still remaining?!,' 29 January.

———— 1948, 'The remnants of *Waesaek* are still there,' 15 August.

———— 1954, 'Strict ban on illegal importation of Japanese-made goods,' 29 March.

———— 1958, 'Smuggling that will ruin the nation,' 2 September.

———— 1960, '[Women's opinion] Should we wear Japanese shoes?,' 17 December.

———— 1963, 'A flood of Japanese culture,' 3 December.

———— 1965a, 'The 'No-buying-Japanese-goods movement,' 30 June.

———— 1965b, 'Massive penetration of Japanese culture,' 11 March.

———— 1966, 'A touchstone for South Korea at the turning-point,' 1 January.

———— 1967, 'Conditional import permission for Japanese cultural films,' 5 August.

———— 1970, 'Children and TV manga films,' 8 May.

———— 1974, 'Monthly Review of Broadcasting,' 30 June.

———— 1975, 'Color television regulation in Busan, Masan, and Ulsan,' 6 November.

———— 1976, 'Editorial: Problematic issues with children's manga,' 7 November.

———— 1979, 'Over 80% of commercially-available cassette tapes unauthorised and defective,' 18 September.

———— 1980, 'Prosperous conditions for illegality: State of the industry seen in amendment,' 24 February.

———— 1981, 'Children contaminated with *waesaek* by lending of Japanese manga,' 26 June.

———— 1988, 'Broadcasting scholar advocates operating system readjustment,' 12 June.

———— 1993, 'Editorial: Television's foreign rip-offs,' 29 January.

Cine 21, 2009, 'Live performances: the return of nostalgic legends,' 12 March.

Daehak Shinmun, 1998, '84.1 percent support liberalization of Japanese popular culture,' 11 May.

Dong-A Ilbo, 1946, '*Waesaek* music! Let's get rid of it,' 13 August.

———— 1948, 'Let's exterminate Japanese music!,' 14 October.

———— 1955, 'New cinema,' 27 April.

———— 1960a, 'One set per five households,' 11 May.

——— 1960b, 'From blues to rockabilly,' 12 August.

——— 1960c, 'Advertisement,' 17 October.

——— 1961, 'Editorial: Let's develop an ethos of austerity and hard work,' 23 May.

——— 1962, '"*Waesaek*" frames foreign film standards,' 9 November.

——— 1963a, '"*Waesaek*" and the film world,' 28 January.

——— 1963b, '"Japanese television boom,"' 4 September.

——— 1964a, 'Japan trouble,' 6 February.

——— 1964b, 'A television boom in Busan,' 11 October.

——— 1965, 'Talking from all angles,' 11 November.

——— 1968, '[Calling for] prudent Korea–Japan entertainment exchange,' 11 January.

——— 1970, 'Childish innocence contaminated by *waesaek*,' 22 April.

——— 1971, 'TV children's programs all sloppy manga films,' 17 September.

——— 1973, 'Japanese TV viewership high in Busan,' 23 April.

——— 1974, 'Japanese video spreads to the southern region,' 17 January.

——— 1979a, 'Selling-place for imported merchandise,' 15 February.

——— 1979b, 'VTR exhibition frequent in city-center hotel district,' 20 November.

——— 1981, 'Much viewing of Japanese TV in Busan,' 7 July.

——— 1982, 'Poorly treated children's TV program. How do you make it in a foreign country?,' 4 May.

——— 1986, 'Japanese culture: Entering from behind,' 14 August.

——— 1989, 'U.S. military stationed in Korea (27),' 10 August.

——— 1990, 'Surging Japanese culture and ingrained Japanese language,' 15 August.

——— 1991a, 'What should we do about Japanese culture?,' 2 March.

——— 1991b, 'Shame on the public trustworthiness of the Performance Ethics Committee,' 11 March.

——— 1991c, 'From street to home...the scene of *Waesaek*,' 19 August.

——— 1998, 'Phased liberalization of Japanese popular culture,' 18 April.

——— 2001, 'Most South Korea–Japan joint cultural events cancelled due to distortions in history textbooks,' 18 July.

——— 2002a, 'Chi Myung-Kwan, South Korea–Japan Cultural Exchange Policy Advisory Committee Chair, withdraws protest,' 17 February.

——— 2002b, 'Keep to principles in liberalization of Japanese popular culture,' 18 February.

Hankook Ilbo, 2002, 'What is the acceptance standard for Japanese popular culture on domestic broadcasting?' 2 February.

Hankyoreh, 1988b, 'Campaign to know North Korea properly: Legal amendment sought,' 22 October.

——— 1988b, 'Make Channel 2 Ours,' 26 May.

——— 1988c, 'Japanese popular culture rushing to landing in Korea,' 1 September.

——— 1996, 'Japanese jazz band's first live performance on visit to South Korea,' 9 February.

———— 2003, 'Gaming, film and recording businesses: Fear not to accept Japanese culture,' 18 September.

———— 2005, 'The dirty secret behind the sacred transformation of Hyeonchungsa and the ban on 'A Camellia of a Girl,' 2 February.

Hankyoreh 21, 2004, 'Turn the rudder towards the Korean wave,' 15 September.

JoongAng Ilbo, 1966a, 'Busan, an intensely *waesaek* port,' 13 January.

———— 1966b, 'Wariness towards Japan urged at press roundtable,' 21 January.

———— 1966c, 'Screening of Japanese films permitted,' 4 May.

———— 1967a, 'Ethics committee representatives from each mass media field,' 1 August.

———— 1967b, 'Contents of agreement by agenda items,' 11 August.

———— 1967c, 'TBC has 5% viewership,' 26 August.

———— 1969, 'Japanese Film Opinion Group,' 8 November.

———— 1971a, 'TV,' 17 February.

———— 1971b, 'Unrepentant bad manga,' 16 June.

———— 1971c, 'TV,' 10 August.

———— 1974, 'New production in *Boys' Theater*,' 29 July.

———— 1975a, 'Deluge of Japanese low-quality TV and children's comics,' 5 April.

———— 1975b, '*Mazinger Z* to air,' 7 August.

———— 1975c, 'Weekly TV Review,' 18 October.

———— 1981, 'The problem of pirated versions of the novel Somehow Crystal,' 21 April.

———— 1984a, 'Return to Busan Port,' 26 January.

———— 1984b, 'U.S. considers review of decision on color television dumping,' 8 March.

———— 1984c, 'Japanese culture infiltrating the younger generation,' 9 July.

———— 1985a, 'The Japan–South Korea [Relationship], Twenty Years On,' 27 June.

———— 1985b, 'South Korea–U.S. bilateral agreement,' 14 December.

———— 1986, 'Foreign nationals' copyright protection premature,' 28 May.

———— 1987, 'EC and Japanese liberalization pressure,' 12 March.

———— 1990, 'Request for control of penetration of satellite broadcasting into South Korea,' 21 March.

———— 1991a, 'Strengthening of control of translations of foreign manga for children,' 24 February.

———— 1991b, 'Koreans hate Japan and enjoy Japanese culture,' 3 April.

———— 1992a, 'Anticipation for ROK–China cultural exchange,' 1 September.

———— 1992b, 'Cheong Wa Dae Secretariat,' 25 September.

———— 1993, 'The sinking domestic manga industry,' 22 August.

Kino, 1998, 'Parting Words to Akira Kurosawa, director, 1910–1998,' October.

———— 1999, 'Love Letter, are you well?,' November.

———— 2000 'Ten 1999 South Korean cinema news items that *KINO* readers chose,' January.

Kyunghyang Shinmun, 1947a, 'Persistent *waesaek*,' 12 January.

—— 1947b, 'The latest changes of the base for the new Korea, Busan Port,' 5 April.

—— 1948, 'Protecting entertainment culture,' 27 June.

—— 1952, 'National Liberation Day commemorative events decided,' 12 August.

—— 1959, 'Warning notice that the Department of Education sent to the Guild of Korean Screenwriters,' 12 August.

—— 1960a, 'The spendthrift tribe [whose] public opinion will ruin the nation,' 17 June.

—— 1960b, 'Advertisement,' 18 October.

—— 1960c, 'Before the birth of the new republic and last month (8) Boom in Japanese-style,' 28 December.

—— 1961, 'Drippings (*Yeojeok*),' 24 December.

—— 1962a, 'Japanese television boom in Busan,' 22 October.

—— 1962b, 'Trouble with Waesaek film import recommendation,' 6 November.

—— 1963, 'Drippings (*Yeojeok*),' 27 March.

—— 1964a, 'Japanese television boom,' 5 January.

—— 1964b, 'Most houses have a television antenna,' 15 January.

—— 1964c, 'Gleanings from the political district,' 24 October.

—— 1968a, 'Film advertisement,' 8 July.

—— 1968b, 'Theatre district bustles on first holiday after abolition of entrance exams,' 18 July.

—— 1970, 'Natural color animation, *The Great Adventure of Sonogong*,' 16 April.

—— 1974, '[Calling for] a strict brake on [content] for adult viewing,' 11 December.

—— 1976, 'Full-scale production of SF manga films in South Korea, too,' 2 March.

—— 1979, 'Weekly review of television from the viewing audience,' 6 February.

—— 1981a, 'The video age opens the door to the image of a third video culture,' 5 October.

—— 1981b, 'Hotel saunas are lewd cinemas,' 5 November.

—— 1984, 'Video shock to the entertainment world,' 19 March.

—— 1988, 'Relaxation of forty years of iron control,' 2 June.

—— 1989, 'Film advertisement,' 1 January.

—— 1990, 'Traditional or *waesaek*? Dispute over trot's origins heats up,' 24 August.

—— 1997, '516 regime is an alliance of the pro-Japanese faction and military circles,' 5 July.

—— 1999, 'Film advertisement,' 20 November.

Maeil Business Newspaper, 2001, 'Dreams of South Korean cinema swell,' 10 January.

Maekyung City Life, 2001, 'Why don't Japanese films sell in South Korea?,' 7 June.

Mainichi Shinbun, 1988, 'The first Japanese song on Korean television,' 1 July.

—— 2001. '[YOUkan] South Korea watching. History Textbooks affect the "best relationship ever,"' 24 February.

Monthly Video, 1985a, 'A defense of video culture,' April 1985 Inaugural Issue.

—— 1985b, 'Complete guide to video editing,' August.

—— 1986, 'Videos from the world village: Japan,' May.

OhmyNews, 2002, 'Opposition to Japanese broadcasting liberalization reduces,' 9 August.

Roadshow, 1989, '1980s Japanese films now,' November.

Screen, 1984, 'Overflowing lewd videos,' November.

———— 1988, 'Japanese cinema,' June.

TV Guide, 1981, 'How much does it cost to import a TV program?' 15 August.

———— 1983, 'Manhwa films' 31 December.

Yomiuri Shinbun, 1993, '"Imitated" programs rampant in South Korea,' 3 February.

Yonhap News, 1999, 'Ban on TV advertisements for Japanese film, *Love Letter*,' 23 October.

———— 2001, 'Government executes first stage of reprisals against Japanese historical distortions,' 12 July.

———— 2003, 'Culture Minister Lee Chang-dong [calls] impact of liberalization of Japanese popular culture insignificant,' 11 June.

Appendix: Table of titles

English	Korean	Japanese	chapter
Adventure on Gaboten Island	*Ttolttori Tamheomdae*	Bōken Gabotenjima	2
Adventures of the Monkey King	*Sonogongŭi mohŏm*	*Gokū no daibōken*	4
Alps Story: My Annette	Alp'ŭsŭŭi sonyŏ haidi	*Arupusu monogatari: Watashi no Annetto*	4
April Story	4wŏl iyagi	*Shigatsu monogatari*	6
Astro Boy	*Ujusonyeon Atom*	*Tetsuwan Atomu*	1, 4
Bayside Shakedown		*Odoru daisōsasen*	6
Big Singing and Dancing Contest		*Utatte odotte daigassen*	3
Big-eyed Frog	*Kaeguriwangnu ni*	*Kerokko Demetan*	4
Bittersweet Show, Let's try/show anything		*Horoniga shō nandemo yarimashō*	3
Candy Candy	*Kendi* (1977) / *Deuljangmi Sonyeo Kendi* (1983)	*Kyandi Kyandi*	4
Dragon Ball	Dragon Ball	Dragon Ball	5
Eagle 5	*Doksuri Ou-Hyungjae*	*Kagaku Ninjatai Gatchaman*	4
Fist of the North Star	Puktuŭi kwŏn	*Hokuto no Ken*	5
Galaxy Express 999	*Eunha cheoldo 999*	*Ginga Tetsudō Surī Nain*	4
Gigantor	*Ch'ŏrin28ho*	*Tetsujin 28-go*	4
Golden Bat	*Hwanggŭmbakchwi*	*Ōgon Batto*	4
How Much for the Whole World?		*Sekai marugoto HOW matchi*	5
Humanoid Monster BEM	Yogoein'gan	*Yōkai ningen Bemu*	4
Hurricane	Naeirŭi cho	*Ashita no Jō*	4
Hurricane Boy	*Akira*	*Akira*	6
In the Realm of the Senses	Kamgagŭi cheguk	*Ai no korīda*	6
Leo, Prince of the Jungle	*Millimŭi wangja reo*	*Janguru taitei* (Kimba the White Lion)	4
Magical Princess Minky Momo	*Yosul gongju Mingki* (Magic Princess Minky)	*Mahō no purinsesu Minkī Momo*	4
Mazinger Z	*Mazinger Z*	*Mazinger Z*	2, 4, 5
Marine Boy	Padaŭi wangja marinboi	*Kaitei shōnen Marin*	4
Million Yen Quiz Hunter		*Hyakuman-en kuizu hantā*	5
Morning Dew	Achim Iseul		5

English	Korean	Japanese	chapter
My Neighbor Totoro	Iwutcim thotholo	*Tonari no Totoro*	6
NHK's Proud of My Voice		*NHK nodo jiman*	5
Persia the Magic Fairy	*Saetbyeol gongju*	*Mahō no yōsei Perusha*	4
Planet Mask	*Yuseonggamyeon Piteo*	*Yūsei kamen*	2
Pokémon the Movie: Mewtwo Strikes Back	Kŭkchangp'an p'ok'enmonsŭt'ŏr myuch'ŭŭi yŏksŭp	*Gekijōban poketto monsutā Myūtsū no gyakushū*	6
Prince Planet	*Ujuŭi wangja ppappi*	*Yūsei shōnen Papī*	4
Queen Millennia		*Shin-Taketori Monogatari: Sennen-jō*	4
Railroad Man	Ch'ŏltowŏn	*Poppoya*	6
Ring 2	Ring 2	*Ringu 2*	6
Romance of the Three Kingdoms	Samgukchi	*Sangokushi*	5
Sally the Witch	Yoswulkongcwu saylli	*Mahōtsukai Sarī*	4
Samurai Fiction		*SF samurai fikushon*	6
Shall We Dance?			6
Shoot the Sun	*T'aeyangŭl sswara*	*Taiyō o ute*	4
Somehow Crystal	Ŏtchŏnji k'ŭrisŭt'al	*Nan to naku, kurisutaru*	5
Space Emperor God Sigma	*Robot Sigma*	*Uchū taitei goddo shiguma*	4
Spirited Away	Sen'gwa ch'ihiroŭi haengbangbulmyŏng	*Sen to Chihiro no Kamikakushi*	6
Takeshi's Castle		*Fūn! Takeshi-jō*	5
Tale of Japanese Burglars		*Nippon Dorobō Monogatari*	4
The Adventures of Hutch the Honeybee	*Haech'iŭi mohŏm*	*Konchū Monogatari Minashigo Hatchi*	4
The Ballad of Narayama	*Narayamabushikō*	*Narayamabushikō*	6
The Eel	*Unagi*	*Unagi*	6
The Rough and Ready Cowboy	*Chadori*	*Kōya no shōnen Isamu*	2, 4
Three Space Musketeers	Ujusamch'ongsa	*Zero Tesutā*	2, 4
Tiger Mask	T'aigŏmasŭk'ŭ	*Taiga Masuku*	4
Warm Spring		*Danshun*	4
Welcome Back, Mr. McDonald	Welk'ŏm misŭt'ŏ maektonaltŭ	*Rajio no jikan*	6

Index

www.ingramcontent.com/pod-product-compliance
Lightning Source LLC
Chambersburg PA
CBHW070242290326
41929CB00046B/2335